目　录

The Macat Library
世界思想宝库钥匙丛书

解析斯蒂芬·平克

《人性中的善良天使》

AN ANALYSIS OF

STEVEN PINKER'S

THE BETTER ANGELS OF OUR NATURE

Why Violence Has Declined

Joulia Smortchkova ◎ 著

乔洁◎译

上海外语教育出版社
SHANGHAI FOREIGN LANGUAGE EDUCATION PRESS

CONTENTS

引 言

要点

- 斯蒂芬·平克，生于 1954 年，美籍加拿大人，哈佛大学实验心理学 * 教授，曾撰写出版多部语言与人类心理学方面的学术著作与通俗读物。实验心理学用可量可测的方法对人类思想与行为进行研究，具有一定的科学准确性。

- 《人性中的善良天使》指出在人类历史进程中暴力已经减少，并进一步探究了暴力减少的潜在原因。

- 自 2011 年出版以来，《人性中的善良天使》一直被广泛认为是暴力史及暴力心理学方面最受争议的书籍之一。

斯蒂芬·平克其人

斯蒂芬·亚瑟·平克，《人性中的善良天使：暴力为什么会减少》（2011）一书的作者，1954 年出生于加拿大蒙特利尔一个犹太家庭中。十几岁的时候，平克就说自己是"一个巴枯宁无政府主义 * 的真正信仰者。"[1] 米哈伊尔·巴枯宁 * 是俄国著名的革命家，集体无政府主义 * 的创始人。集体无政府主义是一个政治理论，强调废除国家，生产工具和生产资料均归集体所有。然而，在 1969 年 10 月，平克 15 岁时，由于蒙特利尔的警察罢工事件，平克的反国家倾向就此终结。当时，警察抗议多伦多（加拿大的另一个城市）同行的薪水比他们高。第二天的事件让平克开始反思社会暴力："当法律的强制性消失后，各种各样的暴力行为便蜂拥而出……上午 11：20，第一家银行遭到抢劫……这一决定性的实证性 * 试验让我的政治观点就此坍塌（同时也预示着我此生将成为科学家）。"[2]（实证性试验即建立在观察证据而非理论基础之上的试验）。

斯蒂芬·平克在蒙特利尔的道森学院开始其本科学习生涯，专业是心理学 *（一门研究人类大脑及其对人类行为影响作用的科学）。之后，平克在加拿大麦吉尔大学获得硕士学位，接着在美国哈佛大学获得实验心理学博士学位。目前，平克为哈佛大学约翰斯通家族心理学系教授。但是，平克最初的兴趣领域并非暴力心理学，而是语言学 *——研究语言方方面面的学问。他的第一本专著《语言本能》出版于 1994 年。平克在该书中为美国语言学家诺姆·乔姆斯基 * 的观点进行辩护。乔姆斯基认为，所有人类都通过同一种结构性语言学习方法同语言相"连接"——：换言之，我们生来并非一块"白板"。平克在其他著作中探索了人类心理学及人类心理机能的演进方式，他的这些学术兴趣在《善良天使》中一览无余。

《人性中的善良天使》的主要内容

斯蒂芬·平克在《人性中的善良天使》中指出，人类的暴力随着时间流逝已经减少。尽管许多人觉得世界在 20 世纪变得更加暴力，但平克以为情况恰恰相反。他认为，暴力在增加或者未来暴力会更甚都只是人们的一种*印象*。有这种印象是因为我们倾向于记住那些易于回忆的事情。我们更易于记住那些令我们恐慌的骇人事件，却不容易记住看似更为平常的普通事件。2015 年 9 月，平克在为英国《卫报》撰写的一篇专题文章中说："这就是我们为什么更害怕被鲨鱼吃掉，而不是从楼梯上摔下去，尽管后者更可能致我们于死地。"[3] 他指出，这种倾向受到了乐于展现暴力事件的媒体的利用。因此，我们看到的世界是暴力的，反而看不到它比过去暴力减少的一面。于平克而言，人类历史进程中发生的大量文化演变已经塑造或者仍在塑造着人们的心理。这些变化使得我们无论作为个人还是一个物种都变得没那么暴力了。

平克使用统计数据支撑自己的论点。这些统计数据包括战争中的死亡人数，种族灭绝＊中的死亡人数，历史上其他大规模暴力事件以及抢劫、凶杀案中的死亡人数。⁴ 平克运用以上数据帮助确认了文化与制度在减少暴力过程中发挥了效力。他认为，这些效力源自"人道主义＊启蒙运动"＊思想，一场始于18世纪、给人类生命赋予极高价值的思想文化运动。启蒙运动改变了社会，它所引发的社会变革也改变了人类的心理。平克认为，其结果就是减少了暴力。

《人性中的善良天使》一书有几个目的。首先，平克反对暴力正在增加的观点。他指出，这种普遍存在的观点会产生负面影响：它会促使我们接受在转瞬即逝的危险印象下所做的决定，而不是经过思考和反思后做出的决定。⁵ 为纠正这一观点，平克就暴力减少的确凿证据和事实给出了客观分析。此外，他也明确了促进暴力减少的有力因素，包括民主的传播以及一种不断上升的趋势——将全人类看作同一社会当中的公民。平克还指出道德价值观和审美品位（即什么可能被认为是"美的"或"丑的"）的变化也在推动我们远离暴力，接近和平＊。

《人性中的善良天使》主要采用描述性写作方法。平克讲述了暴力如何减少的故事，从而批驳暴力正在增加的观点。此外，他通过确认历史发展过程中暴力的发展趋势对此观点加以反驳；通过观察历史变化以探究暴力减少的原因。但是，《人性中的善良天使》也有"处方"的＊目的：平克探讨了有可能会在未来应用于进一步减少暴力的规则与工具。

《人性中的善良天使》的学术价值

2011 年出版后，《人性中的善良天使》很快就成为一部有争议的著作。世界所有知名杂志和报纸——如《纽约时报》《纽约客》《卫报》《经济学人》《华尔街日报》《自然》《金融时报》——都对其做出了评论，平克也通过媒体不断重申该书的主要观点。该书不仅是学术界讨论的重要话题，也是政治、经济、社会领域都在热议的话题。

平克的著作有助于重塑社会科学 *（广泛涵盖人类学、心理学、法学和经济学等学科）界关于暴力的争论。该书开启了对暴力史及暴力减少原因研究的新方法，重新唤起了有关暴力的统计研究兴趣，以及引发（或限制）暴力相关因素的研究兴趣。因此，平克在《人性中的善良天使》中所使用的工具及概念分析可以应用于其他的研究领域，从而加深我们对暴力的理解。

从更加广义的角度而言，该著作也受到了学术界之外、关注社会变革的人士之关注。美国著名企业家、慈善家比尔·盖茨 *在其博客中写到：“《人性中的善良天使》是我读过的最重要的书籍之一——不只是今年的，而是有史以来的。”[6]2015 年，马克·扎克伯格 *——社交网络脸书的创始人，在脸书上创建了一个读书俱乐部。《人性中的善良天使》被选为 2015 “年度好书”第二名。这些认可，都说明了《人性中的善良天使》的重要性、它与公众热议的相关度以及它对世界的影响力。

该书产生的影响是双重的：第一，它有助于提高人们对与暴力相关的最紧迫问题的认识；第二，平克的分析可以用来寻求暴力问题的解决方案：帮助我们制定政策，从而培育和强化在未来可能进一步减少暴力的社会趋势和风气。

1、2. 斯蒂芬·平克：《人性中的善良天使：暴力为什么会减少》，伦敦：企鹅图书，2011 年，第 331 页。

3. 斯蒂芬·平克："好消息：世界真的在改善"，《卫报》，2015 年 11 月 9 日，登录日期 2015 年 12 月 19 日，http://www.the guardian.com/commentisfree/2015/sep/11/news-isis-syria-headlines-violence-steven-pinker。

4. 平克：《善良天使》：第 1—31 页。

5. 平克：《善良天使》：第 xxi 页。

6. 比尔·盖茨："我的书架：《人性中的善良天使：暴力为什么会减少》"，2012 年 6 月 18 日，登录日期 2015 年 12 月 29 日，http://www.gatesnotes.com/Books/The-Better-Angles-of-Our-Nature。

第一部分：学术渊源

1 作者生平与历史背景

要点 ⚷⇒

- 《人性中的善良天使》对暴力趋势的相关统计数据进行了综合回顾。

- 该书指出近几个世纪暴力已经趋于减少，并大胆提出了导致暴力减少的可能原因。

- 20 世纪后半叶是一段较长的和平时期。斯蒂芬·平克成长在这一时期，因此，这可能对他认为暴力减少的观点产生了一定影响。

为何要读这部著作？

斯蒂芬·平克《人性中的善良天使：暴力为什么会减少》在2011 年出版之初便引发争议。该书探讨了 3 个关键主题：

- 暴力史
- 暴力的心理学 * 渊源
- 影响暴力的制度及文化变化

平克认为，暴力已经在历史发展进程中有所减少，这一趋势可能继续下去："尽管世界上仍然存在种种暴力，但我们生活在一个非凡的时代……不管未来趋势如何发展，某种超凡之物已经将我们带到了现在。"[1] 平克为这一乐观前景进行了有力论证，并使用大量数据支撑其论点。因此，这本书集合众多发人深省的思想，由平克严谨的科学方法论 * 支撑，从而具有了重要地位。

《人性中的善良天使》对暴力的相关讨论所产生的影响是不可

否认的。所有知名报纸，如《纽约客》《纽约时报》《卫报》《金融时报》都对该书发表了评论。[2]同时，该书还引发了广泛的学术讨论与公众热议。就其目前的出版状况而言，预言它对学术研究具有长期影响为时尚早，但它对当前争议的重要性却可以通过已有的媒体文献数量给予评定。一旦暴力事件登上报纸头条，记者们便会联系平克以了解其反应。[3]类似事件在 2011 年叙利亚冲突 * 发酵、2013 年乌克兰冲突 * 之初、2015 年对讽刺漫画杂志《查理周刊》* 发生攻击之时都曾有过。2015 年 9 月，平克在英国《卫报》发文阐明自己的观点，尽管这些冲突时有发生，但暴力仍在减少。[4]

> 这本书产生于一个问题的答案："你在乐观什么？"我希望我所收集的数据能够使你不再用传统的悲观态度认识世界的真实状态。
> ——斯蒂芬·平克：《人性中的善良天使：暴力为什么会减少？》

作者生平

斯蒂芬·平克于 1954 年生于加拿大。家中有 3 个孩子，他是老大。平克的父亲是位律师，母亲是一所高中的副校长。他的弟弟目前是加拿大的一位政策分析师 *（工作内容是分析公共政策对社会产生的影响），斯蒂芬·平克和他的妹妹都是心理学家。虽出生于犹太家庭，但平克声称自己是无神论者 *，[5]并批评宗教可能会助长暴力的滋生。

在蒙特利尔的道森学院、麦吉尔大学完成心理学学业后，平克在哈佛大学师从美国心理学家斯蒂芬·科斯林 *，获得实验心理学（用可量可测的方法研究人类思想及行为的学科）博士学位。目前，平克仍然生活在美国，是哈佛大学约翰斯通家族教授。平克有过 3

次婚姻，他的现任妻子是美国小说家丽贝卡·戈尔德斯坦 *。平克承认丽贝卡对《人性中的善良天使》有一定影响，尤其是让他注意到了启蒙运动 6 的重要性。启蒙运动是植根于 18 世纪欧洲的一场思想文化运动，其特征是寻求理性，维护自由、宽容与权利。

《人性中的善良天使》出版之前，平克因其在心理学（研究人类思想及行为的学科）和语言学（研究语言的本质、历史及功能的学科）领域的著作而闻名。平克出版了大量学术著作与通俗读物。这些著作有助于人们对认知科学 *（科学地探索人类大脑与思想的运作、历史及机能的学科）的研究成果产生更大的兴趣，如语言的起源以及我们的认知能力如何发挥作用。平克所接受的科学训练为其在《善良天使》中所使用的统计方法打下了坚实基础，这一科学方法 * 有助于支撑、加强他在书中的论点。

创作背景

我们每天都会听到关于冲突、战争、凶杀以及抢劫的新闻。20世纪前半叶发生过两次世界大战 * 和几次种族灭绝事件 *。因此，人们普遍认为 20 世纪是人类历史上最具毁灭性的时期：真正的全球冲突时代，战争的毁灭性在此达到了新高度。21 世纪初，诸如气候变化 * 和恐怖主义 * 的现代危机开始涌现。我们周围的世界由于地域冲突、宗教极端主义和自然灾害变得四分五裂，因此很多分析家警告我们要小心时代危机：这些警告被媒体无限放大。英国记者罗杰·科恩 * 就写道："我们无比脆弱且充满恐惧。"7

平克出生在 20 世纪中期，这一时期的历史对他关于暴力的认识有一定影响。平克并不认同主流观点——人类比以往更具毁灭性了，相反他完全反对这一观点。他的统计分析表明结论可能完全不同。平克在科学心理学及世俗教育所接受的训练帮助他形成勇于挑战某些观点的习惯。他的出发点在于努力从客观的视角看待人类历史。这就促使他提出以下问题："为什么过去存在那么多暴力？""为什么现在暴力减少了？"平克说："这就是一直敦促我前进的两个心理学问题。"[8]

1. 斯蒂芬·平克：《人性中的善良天使：暴力为什么会减少》，伦敦：企鹅图书，2011 年，第 480 页。

2. 斯蒂芬·平克："《人性中的善良天使》评论节选"，登录日期 2015 年 12 月 29 日，http://stevenpinker.com/content/review-excerpts-better-angels-our-nature。

3. 斯蒂芬·平克："自《人性中的善良天使》出版以来，暴力减少的趋势是否开始逆转"，登录日期 2015 年 12 月 29 日，http://stevenpinker.com/files/pinker/files/has_the_decline_of_violence_reversed_since_the_better_angels_of_our_natur_was_written.pdf?m=1410709356。

4. 斯蒂芬·平克："好消息：世界真的在改善"，《卫报》，2015 年 11 月 9 日，登录日期 2015 年 12 月 19 日，http://www.theguardian.com/commentisfree/2015/sep/11/news-isis-syria-headlines-violence-steven-pinker。

5. 史蒂夫·保尔森："骄傲的无神论者"，《沙龙》，2007 年 10 月 15 日，登录日期 2015 年 12 月 29 日，http://www.salon.com/2007/10/15/pinker_goldstein/。

6. 斯蒂芬·平克："就《人性中的善良天使：暴力为什么会减少》被频繁问及的问题"，登录日期 2015 年 12 月 29 日，http://stevenpinker.com/pages/frequently-asked-questions-about-better-angels-our-nature-why-violence-has-declined。

7. 罗杰·科恩："恐惧气氛"，《纽约时报》，2014 年 10 月 27 日，登录日期 2015 年 12 月 29 日，http://www.nytimes.com/2014/10/28/opinion/roger-cohen-a-climate-of-fear.html。

8. 人类安全报告项目，"全球暴力减少：现实还是神话？"，2014 年 3 月 3 日，登录日期 2015 年 12 月 29 日，http://www.hsrgroup.org/docs/Publications/HSR2013/HSR_2013_Press_Release.pdf。

2 学术背景

要点 ☗━

- 暴力研究是一个复杂的跨学科领域。多个学科的研究者都对这一领域充满兴趣，这些研究者来自人类学 *（通过研究文化、社会和信仰研究人类的学科）、历史学、社会学 *（研究社会功能和社会行为的学科）、经济学 *、政治学 *（研究政治体制和政治行为的学科）、心理学 *（研究人类思想和行为的学科），以及道德哲学 *（研究"正确行为"之本质及伦理的学科）。

- 不同学科的研究者关注的是暴力的不同方面，他们的研究兴趣以他们各自的研究领域为基础。有些学者探究暴力的历史发展，有些学者研究暴力的起因，还有一些学者研究暴力的生物学 *渊源。

- 《人性中的善良天使》综合了历史学、人类学以及心理学方面的研究成果。

著作语境

斯蒂芬·平克《人性中的善良天使：暴力为什么会减少》吸收了众多学科的研究成果。该书综合了多位学者对长期以来暴力的发展趋势，暴力、心理学与人类本性之间关系的研究成果。

平克在阅读美国政治学家泰德·罗伯特·古尔 *的作品后，开始对暴力的相关统计数据感兴趣。[1]1981 年古尔曾发布一张图表，说明英格兰的凶杀率在 13 世纪到 20 世纪之间下降了 95%。其他学者也曾收集过关于暴力的统计数据。约书亚·戈尔茨坦 [*2]，美国知名的国际关系学者，曾研究过战争中的罹难者数量；而美国政治学家鲁道夫·拉梅尔*则考察过大屠杀中的遇难者数量。³平克在《人性中的善良天使》中就采用了他们的研究数据和研究方法。

暴力研究主要涉及以下几个问题：

- 如何收集暴力的相关数据？
- 如何界定暴力？
- 是否能从过去的研究中发现暴力的未来发展趋势？
- 暴力是人性中的天生一面还是后天培养（环境，犹指父母培养和抚育）的结果？ ⁴

换言之，人类是生来就具有某种性格与倾向，还是由于自身在家庭教养、社会、文化环境中学到了这些？平克从这一问题出发着手研究，随后又将其他问题列入其中。

平克的统计方法也涉及数据的相关问题：如何收集数据？如何比较一组组数据？收集数据的最佳办法是什么？是否应该研究其他形式的攻击与冲突数据，比如家庭暴力*或监狱服刑率？政治学家、社会学家以及其他学科的学者们当前正在探讨研究者究竟该使用哪些原始资料⁵。

> 我的早期作品主要反映了我对人性及其对道德与政治影响的兴趣……后来，在 2007 年，由于一系列奇怪事件，不同学科的很多学者联系我，告诉我还有很多证据表明暴力在减少，这些证据比我想象的要多很多。他们的数据使我坚信暴力减少这一主题完全值得写一本书。
>
> ——斯蒂芬·平克："就《人性中的善良天使：暴力为什么会减少》被频繁问及的问题"

学科概览

关于先天与后天*相互作用的讨论由来已久。17世纪的英国哲学家托马斯·霍布斯*（1588—1679）认为，人类天生具有相互打斗的倾向。他说只有出现强大的国家（"利维坦*"）才能阻止无休止战争。[6]相比而言，18世纪出生于日内瓦的哲学家让·雅克·卢梭*（1712—1778）的成就在于发展了"高贵的野蛮人"*理论：当人类生活在自然状态*（群居或以部落为生存单位，而不是一个国家）中时，其本质是善良的。[7]

这些思想家仍然影响着当代人类学、社会学以及心理学。像苏格兰外交官约翰·克劳福*等早期人类学家就受到"高贵的野蛮人"影响。这一影响现在仍然在持续渗透到其他研究领域。[8]其他思想家，如美国科学家和历史学家贾德·戴蒙*则追随霍布斯，强调自然状态下的残暴。这部分学者倾向于认为不按国家方式组织的社会，其特征就是永远生活在冲突当中。心理学界也存在同样的分歧。对于经验主义者*（认为知识仅来源于经验）而言，人生来就是一块"白板"——我们所有的心理机能，包括暴力，都是通过后天的"培养"所获得的。与此相反，先天论者*认为人生来即具有某些机能、能力以及大量知识。

平克在《人性中的善良天使》中站在了霍布斯、戴蒙和先天论者一边。但平克又和霍布斯不一样，他认为人性并非本来邪恶或不可改变，人性中既包括暴力行为也包括和平行为的心理起源。他也并不认为国家是可以减少暴力的唯一一实体。平克认为，暴力减少可以追溯到人类生命价值态度的转变。这一转变始于文化上对理性与自由的强调，这二者是18世纪的思想文化潮流——启蒙运动的结果。

学术渊源

平克的灵感并非源自某一成熟的思想流派，而是源自一群思想家；他们的思想并非紧密相连，却具有共同内核。他承认，两个完全不同的人物对他产生了最为重要的影响：一位是英国数学家刘易斯·弗雷·理查森*，一位是生于德国的社会学家*诺伯特·埃利亚斯*。

刘易斯·理查森是应用数学家（大致就是为实际应用开展研究的数学家），主要以关于天气预报的著作而闻名。他也是最早倡导使用数学分析研究武装暴力的学者之一。[9] 平克采用理查森的统计分析方法来探究暴力史。

平克从诺伯特·埃利亚斯那里继承了他对历史的看法。在著作《文明化进程》中，埃利亚斯指出，自中世纪*结束以来，欧洲的文明化进程不断加快，人们对待暴力行为态度的变化、社会联系的不断加强、自控力的不断增强都可以证明这一点。埃利亚斯确认正是这些力量推动了文明化进程，同时认为文明化进程使人类心理发生了变化。[10]

跟随埃利亚斯的脚步，平克努力探索导致人类心理变化、使人类变得不太暴力的外在因素。他认为思想与社会体制逐渐融为一体，进而开始影响人类的心理。[11] 这种文化与认知心理学*（研究思想、创造力与记忆等思想过程）的融合使得平克将先天与后天重新放到一起来讨论。

1. 斯蒂芬·平克：《人性中的善良天使：暴力为什么会减少》，伦敦：企鹅图书，2011 年，第 60 页。

2. 约书亚·戈尔茨坦：《赢得战争的战争：全球武装冲突的衰落》，纽约：达顿出版社，2011 年。

3. 鲁道夫·拉梅尔：《政府死亡》，新泽西州新不伦瑞克：学报出版社，1994 年。

4. 尼尔斯·佩特·格莱迪奇等："论坛：战争的消亡"，《国际研究评论》第 15 卷，2013 年第 3 期，第 396—419 页。

5. 格莱迪奇等："论坛"，第 396—419 页。

6. 托马斯·霍布斯：《利维坦》，牛津：克拉伦登出版社，2012 年。

7. 让·雅克·卢梭：《论不平等的起源》，富兰克林·菲利普译，牛津：牛津世界经典，2009 年。

8. 泰德·艾灵森：《高贵野蛮人的神话》，伯克利：加利福尼亚大学出版社，2001 年。

9. 刘易斯·弗雷·理查森：《致命争吵统计》，匹兹堡：黄杨出版社，1960 年。

10. 诺伯特·埃利亚斯：《文明化进程》，艾德蒙·杰夫科特译，纽约：众神殿图书，1982 年。

11. 平克：《善良天使》，第 694—696 页。

3 主导命题

要点 🔑

- 思想家们研究暴力时围绕的核心问题是：暴力会随着时间的流逝减少吗？或者说，人类天性是否与暴力本能联系过深而无法改变？

- 斯蒂芬·平克持有积极的世界观，他认为暴力一直在减少，并通过对历史进程中犯罪、战争以及其他暴力事件的统计分析来支撑自己的论点。

- 平克还就暴力为什么会减少，如何减少提出了自己的一套理论。

核心问题

斯蒂芬·平克《人性中的善良天使：暴力为什么会减少》的核心问题就是暴力为*什么*会减少。虽然证明暴力在减少的数据占据了该书最长的章节，但平克关注的并不仅仅是这一下降趋势，而是导致这些变化的原因。他认为，尽管人类心理上有参与冲突的倾向，但他们也拥有制止冲突的心理能力。此外，平克还探索了导致暴力减少的环境、社会因素，尽管目前仍存在某种攻击倾向。

平克并非首位关注暴力历史发展趋势的思想家。他说自己对这一领域的兴趣是受加拿大进化心理学家＊马丁·戴利＊和马戈·威尔逊＊著作的启发。（进化心理学从现代进化理论的角度研究人类和非人类的心理。）在《杀人》（1988）一书中，戴利和威尔逊指出，暴力致死在历史进程中已经减少。最近，这个命题已经被人们更加广泛地讨论和接受了。[1]

然而倘若将这一观点置于 20 世纪的历史背景下来看，似乎有些违背常理，因为这段时期发生了两次世界大战 *，以及种族灭绝、殖民主义 *（外来强权或民族对一个国家或民族的剥削、统治）以及恐怖主义 * 事件。这些事件导致人们普遍认为，我们生活在世界历史上最暴力的一个时代。平克的这部著作对这一观念直接提出了挑战。其原创性在于，平克认为暴力减少可追溯至我们价值观和制度的改变。反过来，这些变化也影响了人类的心理。

> 让自己可怕的想象决定自己对未来可能性的感知是非常愚蠢的……这些数字告诉我们，战争、种族灭绝和恐怖主义在过去 20 年中都有所减少——虽然没有减少到零，但已经减少了很多……很多支持这一可喜结果的条件——民主、繁荣、顺民意的政府，对和平的维护，开放的经济以及反人类意识形态的减少——当然都不可能保证它们永远持续下去。但它们也不可能一夜之间消失。
>
> ——斯蒂芬·平克：《人性中的善良天使：暴力为什么会减少》

参与者

暴力问题是许多政治、社会议题的核心，也是诸多不同领域学者的关注点。历史学家乐于研究暴力相关的数值数据，如法国历史学家罗伯特·穆切布尔德致力于研究从中世纪 * 晚期到今天的暴力发展趋势，并设法找到其减少的根源。像平克一样，他也对男性攻击性是如何得到制服的十分感兴趣，并指出这也是暴力减少的原因之一。[2]

人类学家已经研究了暴力问题的许多方面，诸如它在人类族谱中的起源以及在不同社群中的发展，[3] 而进化心理学家则试图找到暴力的生物学与心理学起源。此外，进化心理学家还研究致力于减少冲突的机制（如道德）。[4] 美国的夫妻档研究者约翰·图比 * 和勒达·科斯米德斯 * 是进化心理学界的开创者。他们已经对人类"天性"如何与人类从现代社会学到的思维模式相互作用或产生碰撞进行了详细研究。

以上仅是广阔研究领域与公众讨论参与者中的少量范例。尽管存在多种声音，但争论本身的核心仍然是那些极少被重复的主张与观点。

当代论战

现如今的研究大概有两种普遍争议。第一种与数字相关：暴力究竟在增加还是减少？第二种是与暴力起源相关：暴力究竟来自于人类的生物性还是来自于社会？

有一种观点将暴力单单归因于社会。平克志在反驳这一观点。2000 年，也就是《人性中的善良天使》出版前 11 年，他曾为《纽约时报》撰写过一篇文章，文中这样写道："许多知识分子普遍认为——邪恶与人性没有丝毫关系，完全是政治体制作用的结果。"[5]

平克不断质疑上述观点。他指出暴力是人性的一部分。但同时，他又设法找到中间地带以避免这一观点所产生的否定结论。平克认为，如果暴力是人性的一部分，则可以为历史和社会所驯服。他指出，启蒙运动的理性思想点即为这种可能性的关键。这一观点与英国理论物理学家大卫·多伊奇 * 相似，用平克的话来说，多伊奇"捍卫了一个过时的观点——启蒙运动开启了一个无限睿智和道德进步的时代。"[6]

1. 如，约翰·穆勒："战争已经不复存在：一项评估"，《政治科学季刊》第 124 卷，2009 年第 2 期，第 297—321 页。

2. 罗伯特·穆切布尔德：《中世纪晚期到今天的暴力史》，剑桥：政治出版社，2012 年。

3. 贝蒂娜·施密特和因戈·施罗德：《暴力与冲突人类学》，纽约：心理学出版社，2001 年。

4. 约翰·托比和勒达·科斯米勒斯："思想中的群体：战争与道德的联动根源"，载《人类道德与社会性：进化与比较视角》，亨利克·霍夫-奥里森编，纽约：帕尔格雷夫麦克米伦出版社，2010 年，第 91—234 页。

5. 斯蒂芬·平克："一切邪恶"，《纽约时报》，2000 年 10 月 29 日，登录日期 2015 年 12 月 22 日，http://www.nytimes.com/2000/10/29/books/all-about-evil.html。

6. 斯蒂芬·平克："斯蒂芬·平克：照章办事"，《纽约时报：周日书评》，2014 年 9 月 25 日，登录日期 2015 年 12 月 22 日，http://www.nytimes.com/2014/09/28/books/review/steven-pinker-by-the-book.html。

4 作者贡献

要点 🗝

- 平克对暴力起源持中立态度。他指出，人类心理有驱向于暴力的某些方面，但文化与制度因素能够抑制这些倾向。

- 平克调动多方数据研究过去和现在暴力的不同程度。

- 平克适度的回答为先天—后天＊之争提供了一个较为恰当的观点：尽管暴力是人性的一部分，外界的因素（后天养育）也能对它产生影响。

作者目标

在《人性中的善良天使：暴力为什么会减少》一书中，斯蒂芬·平克旨在质疑关于暴力和人性的两种假设。一是暴力在历史发展进程中持续稳定增长；[1] 二是我们应该对人类境况持消极态度。平克指出，尽管我们生来具有某些倾向——一种人类心理的内在生物内核——但这并不意味着我们注定会回归暴力。他挑战了"对人性的信念与人类境遇的宿命论之间的平衡"。[2]

平克首先通过数据概览，为暴力心理与暴力史之间的相互作用绘制了一幅复杂但条理清晰的图纸。随后，又探究了可能鼓励暴力或抑制暴力的心理因素。最后，他综合以上研究指出，历经几个世纪，人类暴力已经减少，且这种减少得益于外界因素。正是这些外界因素驯服了人类的暴力倾向——但并没有彻底消灭它。这一方法使得平克需要根据内部因素（心理的）和外部因素（制度和文化的）之间复杂的相互作用，对暴力起源与暴力减少的相关问题进行重新界定。

平克在《人性中的善良天使》中部分实现了自己的目标。他通过统计数据所呈现的暴力发展趋势尽管存在争议，但的确表明暴力有所减少。他关于历史与心理之间相互作用的观点——尽管也存在争议——的确合乎一定的逻辑。

> 对于关注人性的任何一个人而言，这都是一个自然形成的话题。"人类这一物种是天生暴力好战还是热爱和平、喜欢合作？"这一问题实际上得回溯到几百年前，甚至几千年前。因此，自然就落到心理学的范畴之内……大家的担忧在于：如果基因中存在暴力——如果我们是杀人猿，我们DNA中具有谋杀因子——那么你将无计可施。但这一推论并不合理。真正的答案是"不"，我们不必听天由命。
>
> ——斯蒂芬·平克：《怀疑探索者》采访

研究方法

平克在《人性中的善良天使》中采用了科学分析的方法。他从定义出发，对收集的大量数据进行检验，然后根据自己的命题对这些数据进行解释。平克将"暴力"界定为对他人造成伤害的任何一种物理的力量，不包括隐喻性暴力，如语言攻击。平克对两类物理暴力的相关数据进行了检验：一类是公民的个人行为（凶杀、抢劫、袭击等等）；一类是制度行为（战争、种族灭绝、死刑以及其他类似的情况）。

平克的数据来自许多不同渠道：法医考古学*（即基于犯罪现场分析方法的考古学）、人种学*（对文化的研究）、城市档案、乌普萨拉冲突数据计划*和奥斯陆和平研究所（具有分别由瑞典和挪威主持发布的资料，这些资料为了解暴力和冲突解决提供了非常有用的统计和分析数据。）有时候，平克会使用历史学家和政治学家研究战争和种族灭绝的相关数据。他对数据选择非常严格，声称其目的"就是只使用那些确保客观来源的数据。"[3] 值得注意的是，平克计算的是暴力犯罪的相对比率而非绝对数值。换言之，他计算的是暴力受害者占一定人口数量的比例。尽管现在的暴力死亡人数比过去多，但这一数字需要与人口总数作比。平克指出，一旦将后者考虑在内，现在的暴力死亡人数就比过去少很多。

最后，平克采用哲学、社会学以及心理学的理论观点揭露由数据揭示的更大趋势，其中最主要的是德国社会学家诺伯特·埃利亚斯的著作。平克采用埃利亚斯《文明化进程》中的理论探究引发暴力减少的社会原因。

时代贡献

就其广度、复杂性及跨学科（采用不同学科的目的与方法）的本质而言，《人性中的善良天使》具有极高的独创性。平克借用军事历史学家和社会学家的方法收集暴力的相关数据，他随后采用进化心理学*的方法来研究历史上暴力发展趋势是如何与人类心理学如何联系在一起的。

这部作品的独创性还来自于平克将概念性命题和实证性数据（即通过观察可以验证的数据）相结合的能力：

- 尽管历史学家在收集指向暴力减少的数据，但他们并未做出这一趋势的心理阐释。
- 心理学家正在研究暴力的生物学渊源以及可以改变这些因素

的方法。

- 一些道德哲学家＊认为人类已经取得道德进步，但他们的结论并没有数据基础。

平克在《人性中的善良天使》中设法将以上所有的研究线索综合在一起形成了逻辑清晰的论点。

尽管平克已经成为认知科学＊（主要利用哲学、神经科学和语言学等学科方法研究大脑与思想的跨学科领域）领域的一员，但他更多将自己定位为一个严格意义上不属于任何一个思想学派的独立思想家。尽管如此，他也承认自己受惠于许多理论家，受到"人道主义启蒙运动"＊的启发，这是一种基于科学、世俗而理性的研究方法。

---

1. 斯蒂芬·平克：《人性中的善良天使：暴力为什么会减少》，伦敦：企鹅图书，2011 年，第 xxi—xxv 页。
2. 斯蒂芬·平克："就《人性中的善良天使：暴力为什么会减少》被频繁问及的问题"，登录日期 2015 年 12 月 29 日，http://stevenpinker.com/pages/frequently-asked-questions-about-better-angels-our-nature-why-violence-has-declined。
3. 斯蒂芬·平克："被频繁问及的问题"。

第二部分：学术思想

5 思想主脉

要点 ⚷

- 平克以我们拥有"五个心魔和四个天使"来总结人类暴力与和平天性的心理 * 根源。
- 他将我们的"四个天使"界定为同理心 *、自制、道德感和理性。
- 平克之所以使用数据和统计结果是因为他希望为暴力现象提供客观分析。

核心主题

斯蒂芬·平克在《人性中的善良天使：暴力为什么会减少》一书中指出，暴力在人类历史进程中已经减少——这一主张与目前流行的暴力增长说形成鲜明对比。如平克所述："我必须让大家相信，暴力在历史发展进程中已经减少，但也知道这一观点势必会引发质疑、不相信，有时甚至是愤怒。"[1] 他说，要到达这一目的，只有坚实可靠的证据才能发挥作用，"我必须用数字说服大家。"[2]

暴力减少一说既适用于大规模暴力（国家之间、民族之间的冲突），也适用于小规模暴力（家庭之间、社群之间的冲突）。平克对这一趋势进行了跨越千年、极具广度的历史回顾。他从史前狩猎采集者 *（靠狩猎和采集而不是靠发展农业生活的人类）开始自己宏伟的历史调查，然后转向中世纪 *，以十分具有说服力的方式指出中世纪 * 社会充满了暴力。接着，他继续对当代社会的研究，声称尽管 20 世纪发生了两次世界大战 *，但暴力在这一时期仍然有所减少。

随后，平克开始探索人类心理学，试图揭示使我们变得更加和平的力量。他明确其中有两种相对的心理因素：我们受"心魔"的推动走向暴力，又受"人性中善良天使"（出自 19 世纪美国总统亚伯拉罕·林肯 *）的敦促而互相协作、和平共处。据平克所言，心理学显示人类既非性本善也非性本恶。相反，"人性中包含了推动我们走向暴力的动机……当然也有推动我们走向和平的动机。"[3]

在该书的最后一部分，平克将历史与心理学加以综合，探究了已经改变（或正在改变）人类心理的外界因素。

> 经过时间长河的流逝，暴力已经减少。今天我们生活在人类这一物种诞生以来最为和平的年代……暴力的历史轨迹不仅影响人们怎样生活，也会影响人们怎样理解生活。人类的长期斗争是让我们更加美好还是更加糟糕，对于我们而言，理解其目的与意义与理解其概念，哪一个更为基本？
>
> ——斯蒂芬·平克：《人性中的善良天使：暴力为什么会减少》

思想探究

平克列出导致暴力减少的 6 大历史转折，其中最重要的是以下两点：

- "文明化进程" *——借用生于德国的社会学家诺伯特·埃利亚斯的术语，表示始于中世纪的一系列制度、价值观和感性变化，从而帮助创建更加平和的社会态度。
- "人道主义革命"——18 世纪欧洲出现由启蒙运动所开创的和平主义 *、包容以及现世主义文化。

除以上两种基本的历史性力量之外，平克还指出其他 4 种有助于减少暴力的趋势：

- 自第二次世界大战＊结束以来战争在欧美国家已经消失；
- 过去 30 年来全世界范围内冲突的减少；
- 经济稳定。

之后平克考察了心理因素。他明确指出其中两种相对的因素：驱使我们走向暴力的"五个心魔"和引导我们走向和平与合作的"四个天使"。平克指出，从心理学的角度而言，"攻击"并不是一种整体现象而是源自五种不同的心理因素（即所谓的心魔）。"四个天使"是使我们加强合作，促进利他主义和无私行为的心理素养：即同理心、自制、道德观和理性。

在研究历史与心理的相互作用时，平克指出有五种因素塑造了人类的心理并且正在促进暴力减少：

- 强国（就政府意义而言）的出现，对暴力行动能进行有效控制（例如，通过警力或军队）；
- 国际商务的发展，要求和平交流与稳定；
- 对女性的尊重不断提高，有时甚至被认为是女性主义＊价值观；
- 现代交通工具及通讯工具的涌现；
- 对合理、理性观点的重视

所有这些因素一起鼓励人类去倾听他们的"善良天使"、缄默他们的"心魔"。

语言表述

《人性中的善良天使》做了极好的研究。平克在广泛调查，在大量事实、图表和数据的基础上得出了结论。尽管如此，该书亲切易读、通俗易懂，或者用平克自己的话来说，"时不时地，有些无礼"。[4]这本书不仅面向专业读者，更多是为了呈现给普通大众。平克希望能够拥有大量读者，同时也能对当前研究暴力的学者们产生影响，从而促进学术争论与研究。

不过，作品中的确使用了统计工具，所以没有接受过任何统计学训练的读者也许不能完全理解数据的收集和分析方法。但是经过书中的一再解释、讨论，这些统计数据还是相当易懂的。正如平克所言："我必须用数字说服大家，我会从数据集合中收集数字并将其在图表中描绘出来。我会解释每一个案例中的数字来源，并尽我所能阐释他们的排列方式。"[5]

书中采用口语化的语言，使用逸闻趣事，有时取自平克本人的生活经历（比如，他说这本书就是一个故事，里面有"六种趋势、五个心魔、四个善良天使和五种历史力量"[6]），这就使得整个论点容易被理解和接受。

---

1. 斯蒂芬·平克:《人性中的善良天使：暴力为什么会减少》，伦敦：企鹅图书，2011年，第 xxii 页。
2. 平克:《人性中的善良天使》，第 xxii 页。

3. 平克：《人性中的善良天使》，第 483 页。
4. 平克：《人性中的善良天使》，第 696 页。
5. 平克：《人性中的善良天使》，第 xxii 页。
6. 平克：《人性中的善良天使》，第 xxiv 页。

6 思想支脉

要点 ⚷

- 《人性中的善良天使》研究了宗教、意识形态*和暴力之间的关系。（意识形态即群体或个人所持有的包含规范、信仰和理论的一个体系。）

- 平克还评价了生理在推动或减少暴力方面发挥的作用。他具体谈到了性别*差异——其作品所产生的争论当中通常被忽略的一个主题。

- 平克关于暴力演进的评价，对进化心理学的相关讨论产生了一定影响。

其他思想

斯蒂芬·平克《人性中的善良天使：暴力为什么会减少》是一部内涵复杂的作品，书中包含大量思想，相互关联；除主要思想外，书中还有很多次要思想。

其中一个重要的次要思想，就是关于宗教在暴力史中所扮演的角色。一些思想家认为基督教*在反暴力方面发挥了重要作用，但平克持反对意见。相反，他关注十字军东征*（中世纪*时期欧洲基督教军队入侵中东地区的战争）和宗教法庭*（基督教会为确保信仰及宗教仪式之纯洁性在 13 世纪设立的一个机构，后来因为其在逼供时所使用的极刑而臭名昭著），以强调其在引发冲突和迫害中所扮演的角色。平克在本书中的主要观点是世俗化*（非宗教化）进程让世俗的民主*自由有所发展，暴力有所减少。书中还有一个关键的次要问题：我们是否已经*进化*为一个不太暴力的物种？平克提出这样一个问题：在一些性状的选择中，是否会优先挑选热爱和平的个体，而不是暴力的个体？或者说多少年来人性是否从未发生任何变化？尽管平克认为有几条证据可能会证明生物进化*改变了核心的人类冲动，但他最终还是否定了这一观点。对此，平克这样解释："尽管从理论上而言，最近的生物进化可能对我们的暴力或非暴力倾向稍有调整，但还没有充分的证据说明它已经产生了这样的作用……至少目前没有，因此，我们没必要做这样的假设。"[1] 平克最终认为在暴力减少的过程中（大约 10,000 年），人类在生理性上没有发生任何变化。

> 当谈到暴力史时，最有意义的事情并非区分有神论制度和无神论政权，而是区分以下两种政权：基于妖魔化的乌托邦意识形态基础上的政权（如纳粹主义*、激进宗教）；基于人权理想的世俗化自由民主政权。
>
> ——斯蒂芬·平克：《人性中的善良天使：暴力为什么会减少？》

思想探究

平克回应说，事实并非如此。这些政权之所以引发暴力，并不是因为它们是无神论的，而是因为他们都在受极权主义意识形态所左右——这些政府以干涉民生、激进地压制异己为政治哲学之要点。换言之，他们受认可其暴力行为的教义所驱动（如纳粹，就是信仰某种形式的种族优越感）。平克指出，大极权主义受教义驱动的本质使他们具有和宗教基本相似的特征。平克继续对比了基于意识形态的政权（宗教和非宗教的）和世俗化的自由民主政权（目前西方世界的主要政体），他认为，世俗化的自由民主体制中暴力有所减少。

尽管平克否认非暴力特征有所进化，但他也在思考人类生理性有多大的可塑性（即，它有多容易被塑造）。这一问题的答案会对人类心理＊的可塑性上产生影响。平克认为，这里存在一定的灵活性，但这种灵活性主要取决于环境在多大程度上更有利于"善良天使"而不是"心魔"。

被忽视之处

《人性中的善良天使》出版后一直被忽略的一个次要思想就是平克所讨论的性别差异与暴力之间的关系。统计数据表明，男性比女性更具有暴力倾向。平克这样写道："一生中睾丸素＊的增加减少或多或少地与男性的好斗＊有所关联。"[2]（好斗指攻击倾向。）

平克认为心理（和生理）因素使男性更具暴力倾向。这并不是说所有男性都很暴力，而是说某些生理因素使得男性在某种社会文化背景下更具有攻击性。由此出发，平克指出，社会的"女性化"已经成为减少暴力的一个因素。他所说的"女性化"指的是"女性特质"（如同理心）所受到的重视以及对女性政治赋权的增加。这种政治赋权有诸如以下几种情况：结束男性伴侣独揽大权的婚姻；女孩享有出生权；女性有权控制生育。

性别问题仍是今天热议的一个话题。平克认同"公平女性主义"＊：要求女性具有和男性平等的法律权利，例如，依照此思想，女性与男性做同样的工作就应该得到同等的报酬。但也指出，不同性别之间存在生理和心理差异。[3]在《白板》（2002）一书中，平克曾写道："男性和女性的思想不可互换……除了权力，人们还拥有欲望……"[4]

平克在《人性中的善良天使》中探讨了性别差异及其在暴力史中所发挥的作用。除了对减少暴力可能采取的措施提供深刻见解，平克的观点对教育等领域也产生了重要影响。

1. 斯蒂芬·平克:《人性中的善良天使：暴力为什么会减少》, 伦敦: 企鹅图书, 2011 年, 第 620—621 页。
2. 平克:《善良天使》, 第 519 页。
3. 斯蒂芬·平克、伊丽莎白·斯皮克:"性别科学与科学, 平克与斯皮克的辩论", 《边缘：第三文化》, 2005 年 5 月 16 日, 登录日期 2015 年 12 月 22 日, Edge.org/3rd_culture/debate05/debate05_index.html。
4. 斯蒂芬·平克:《白板：人性的现代否定》, 伦敦: 企鹅图书, 2002 年, 第 343 页。

7 历史成就

要点 🔑

- 《人性中的善良天使》对悲观的历史观提出了挑战，通过坚实可靠的统计数据说明在人类历史进程中暴力已经减少。

- 该书也致力于探索暴力减少背后的文化和心理*因素。平克在这方面的成就是有争议的。

- 平克的数据问题在于大多数数据都局限于西方世界。

观点评价

　　在撰写《人性中的善良天使：暴力为什么会减少》时，平克有两个明确的目标：一是告诉人们尽管印象中暴力在增加，但实际上随着时间的流逝，暴力在稳定减少；二是揭示暴力减少背后的原因。

　　平克通过令人印象深刻的数据收集整理实现了第一个目标。书中包含从不同来源收集的大约100幅图表[1]。这些图表展示了暴力不仅是小规模暴力（家庭和社会当中），而且大规模暴力（民族和国家之间）也呈现下降趋势。平克还成功解释了人们为什么会认为暴力在增加（尽管这些数据表明暴力在减少）："如果你对世界的认识只基于你所看到的新闻，那么你的观点就会不正确。因为这些新闻描述的都是发生的事情，尤其是不好的事情——鉴于人类的认知本质，人们通常都是通过自己十分容易从记忆中回想出的事例对风险做出评估。"[2]

　　平克的第二目标就是揭示暴力为什么会减少。

他认为这主要归因于文化和制度因素的出现，如民主、贸易的和世界大同主义 * 的发展——世界大同主义认为所有人类都是同一个社会的公民——两者的发展促进了文化与信息交流。这些因素也引发了更加维护和平社会的制度变革。

就这一方面而言，平克的论点只是一种可能性，但还没有得到证实。暴力是一个非常复杂多面的现象。因此，我们缺乏有力的科学证据来证明制度变化对减少暴力产生的影响。但这并不是说平克的论点是错误的。平克认为，暴力减少与某些文化变革*相互关联*（可能还是非常密切的关联）。但他并未能够明确地证实这些变化的确会导致暴力减少。

> 《人性中的善良天使》是极其重要的一部作品。要掌控诸多研究、跨越诸多不同领域，真是一项伟大的成就。平克关于暴力已经急剧下降的证明令人信服，他所提出的关于暴力减少的原因也很有说服力。
>
> ——彼得·辛格：《暴力是历史吗？》

当时的成就

不可否认，《人性中的善良天使》是一个非常成功的商业案例：一本激起热烈讨论的畅销书。它的成功也许是因为选择了 2011 年这个合适的时机出版，与几起广为人知的暴动几乎同时出现：中东地区和北非 2010 年开始的"阿拉伯之春" *，以及恐怖主义领袖奥萨马·本·拉登 * 的死亡：这两起事件似乎——在当时——都是在支持平克的观点。

平克关于暴力减少的论点以实证性 * 数据为基础，即可以观察到的实际信息。与所有真正的实证性论点一样，平克的论点保持着开放性，可以被验错。这就意味着这部作品的有效性和贡献需要后续数据继续支撑。

与此相关的，平克最近又检验了 2011 年到 2015 年间收集的最新数据。结论是："自《人性中的善良天使》完成以来，世界的发展趋势并没有表现出与暴力减少的历史趋向相反的情况，除了叙利亚冲突的影响，其他每一个案例都表明暴力在持续减少。"[3]

尽管有其局限性，《人性中的善良天使》仍然极具贡献。也许对其成就最为中肯的评价当属英国政治学家亚当·罗伯茨 * 的评论："尽管尚有诸多不尽人意之处，（该书）还是称得上有史以来涉及恐怖暴力主题的最有趣作品。它也许是元历史的，但真的很有启发意义。"

局限性

不过，《人性中的善良天使》的确存在一些不足。这在平克数据分析和概念框架中都很显著。

数据方面主要有 3 个问题：

- 平克比较暴力死亡数据的时间范围彼此之间相距甚远，比如 18 世纪和 20 世纪。视这点为问题，是因为我们对过去事件的记录有限，要比较两个差异巨大且时间相隔甚远的时代必须将其建立在过度简化的条件基础之上。
- 平克并非总会将由战争间接引发的死亡考虑在内。澳大利亚学者杰夫·刘易斯 * 对战后死亡率的排除这一点提出质疑。他指出，战争总会引发接踵而来的平民死亡，或是由于生活水平降低，或是由于疾病，或是因为自杀。如果将这些数据包含在内，战争死亡率就会增加。

- 平克的数据集也有地理局限性，主要来自美国和欧洲；世界其他地区基本上被忽略了。美国记者伊丽莎白·科尔伯特*写道："平克关注的范围几乎完全局限在西欧。"[4] 她批评平克并没有讨论植根于殖民主义*（占统治地位的外国强权或民族对一个地区或民族的剥削）的暴力及其对被殖民国家的影响。

该书的另一局限性是平克对暴力的界定：使用任何一种物理的力量对他人造成伤害。他并没有将语言暴力、隐喻暴力和经济暴力包含在内。更为重要的是，他没有将民主国家可能被视为国家暴力的行为包含在内，比如美国监禁率的增长以及对囚犯的虐待。这一局限的定义可能会影响平克论点的适用范围。

---

1. 斯蒂芬·平克："图表证据：试验中的平克乐观主义"，《卫报》，2015 年 9 月 11 日，登录日期 2015 年 12 月 22 日，http://www.theguardian.com/commentisfree/ng-interactive/2015/sep/11/graphic-evidence-steven-pinkers-optimism-on-trial。
2. 斯蒂芬·平克："自《人性中的善良天使》出版以来，暴力减少的趋势是否开始逆转？"，登录日期 2015 年 12 月 22 日，http://stevenpinker.com/files/pinker/files/has_the_decline_of_violence_reversed_since_the_better_angels_of_our_natur_was_written.pdf?m=1410709356。
3. 斯蒂芬·平克："暴力减少的趋势是否开始逆转"。
4. 伊丽莎白·科尔伯特："当代和平：斯蒂芬·平克的暴力史"，《纽约客》，2011 年 10 月 3 日，登录日期 2015 年 12 月 22 日，http://www.newyorker.com/magazine/2011/10/03/peace-in-our-time-elizabeth-kolbert。

8 著作地位

要点 🔑

- 平克的主要作品都在关注是人类心理学*，它的机能以及发展渊源。

- 《人性中的善良天使》是平克的第 13 部作品，也是他畅销作品中最受争议的一部。

- 《人性中的善良天使》以更为广阔的历史文化视野，与平克关于人类心理学功能的研究著作相关联。

定位

2011 年，《人性中的善良天使：暴力为什么会减少》出版的时候，斯蒂芬·平克早已是认知科学领域畅销书作者中最有影响力的一位。《人性中的善良天使》相对于平克的前期作品而言，更是一部鸿篇巨著：因为平克走出自己的专业领域（认知科学*），将心理学与历史学、社会学*以及经济学*融合在一起。他曾在几次采访中都解释说，自己至少从 2007 年就开始思考《善良天使》中所谈及的问题了。书中主题与他早先探讨人性的两本书相关：一本是《白板：人性的现代否定》（2002），另一本是《思想本质：语言是洞察人类天性之窗》（2007）。[1]

尽管在过去的 4 年中，平克不断探讨书中相关问题，但《善良天使》之后，他还是没有再写出暴力主题的重要作品。平克的最新作品是《风格感觉：21 世纪写作指南》（2014）。如题目所示，该书旨在帮助人们找到一种清楚且易读的写作风格。这偏离了平克之前探讨的主题，但又如他的早期作品一般，《风格感觉》受到了心理学和自然科学最新研究的深刻启示。

> 人性是包含很多因素的复杂体系。它既包含引导我们走向暴力的心智能力，也包含让我们远离暴力的心智能力，如同理心、自制和公正感。同时也配备无限的语言与理性的组合能力，这些能力让我们反思自己的处境，找到生活的更好方式。这种对于心理学的愿景和对现世人文主义的投入在我书中是不变的主题，不过近年来这点于我已经越发清楚了。
>
> ——斯蒂芬·平克：就《人性中的善良天使：暴力为什么会减少》被频繁问及的问题

整合

平克的职业生涯主要关注人类心理学及其在自然与社会中的地位。《人性中的善良天使》对此进行了延伸，将人类心理学问题置于更加广阔的历史语境中。就此而言，该书便成为他最宏大的著作之一。

平克的早期作品着眼于实验心理学*（使用科学的方法研究人类思想和行为）与语言学*（研究在语言界定中同时发挥作用的各种事物）。他与美国认知科学家斯蒂芬·科斯林*合作研究心理意象（我们向自己表述世界的方式）和三维空间的表现形式。之后，平克关注婴儿在语言学习过程中如何习得不规则动词。他关于这方面的研究在其著作《词与规则：语言成分》（1999）得到了普及。[2]

那时，平克已经出版了两本畅销书。一本是《语言本能》（1994），将美国语言学家诺姆·乔姆斯基*的语言研究作品介绍给普通大众。乔姆斯基认为，语言的规则是内在的：学习只能激发头脑中已经存在和储存的内容。平克以此反驳并持与之相反的观点：人生来是一块干净的白板，语言是从外部植入的社会构建。

1997年，平克出版了另外一本畅销书：《心智探奇》。这本书与《白板：人性的现代否定》（2002）、《思想本质：语言是洞察人类天性之窗》总体来说更加关注心理学。它们为普通大众介绍了当代实验认知科学和进化心理学*的思想。

《白板》一书预见到了一些《人性中的善良天使》中讨论的问题。平克在该书中否定了以下观点：思想是一幅空白的画布，等待文化与社会的塑造填充。他认为，思想受进化*过程塑造，然后定型。社会改变思想的能力是有限的："否定人性已经延伸到学术界之外的领域，引发了精神生活与常识的脱节。"[3] 平克在《人性中的善良天使》中再次探讨了进化与心理学之间的关系。

意义

《人性中的善良天使》使平克成为当代最有影响力的思想家之一。鉴于平克所涉足研究的主题和领域之多样，很难说该书是他的最佳作品或最重要的作品。比如说，很难将这本书与他的心理意象研究或儿童习得不规则动词的学术研究作比。但可以肯定的一点是，虽然凭借其心理学领域的科学著作和通俗读物，平克已成为人所共知的一名认知科学家，《人性中的善良天使》却使他成为一名具有全球影响力的思想家。事实上，2013 年，平克被《前景》杂志评为"年度最有影响力的思想家"第三位。如英国记者约翰·达格代尔所述："也许平克只是很好地绘制了图表，可真正使他名声大震的也许是他从心理语言学的专业领域向《人性中的善良天使》中历史学角度的转变。"[4] 2014 年，平克在美国双月刊《外交政策》评选出的全球最顶尖的 100 位思想家中居第二十六位。[5]

正如这些评论所说，《人性中的善良天使》使平克在其最初专业领域之外名声大噪，成为时下热点问题相关讨论的核心人物。

1. 斯蒂芬·平克："就《人性中的善良天使：暴力为什么会减少》被频繁问及的问题"，登录日期 2015 年 12 月 15 日，12 月 22 日，http://stevenpinker.com/pages/frequently-asked-questions-about-better-angels-our-nature-why-violence-has-declined。

2. 斯蒂芬·平克：《词与规则：语言成分》，纽约：哈勃柯林斯出版公司，1999 年。

3. 斯蒂芬·平克，《白板：人性的现代否定》，伦敦：企鹅图书，2002 年，第 14 页。

4. 约翰·达格代尔："理查德·道金斯在民测中获世界顶尖思想家"，《卫报》，2013 年 4 月 23 日，登录日期 2015 年 12 月 22 日，http://www.theguardian.com/books/booksblog/2013/apr/25/richard-dawkins-named-top-thinker。

5. 《外交政策》，"纷争的世界：2014 全球顶尖思想家"，登录日期 2015 年 12 月 30 日，http://globalthinkers.foreignpolicy.com。

第三部分：学术影响

9 最初反响

要点 ⚷—

- 关于《人性中的善良天使》的反应有点两极分化。负面评论要么怀疑平克的概念假设，要么质疑他对数据的使用和阐释。

- 平克在期刊文章或者相关采访中，以不同方式对以上部分批评做出了回应，或通过展示更多数据，或通过重申其概念要点。

- 很多批评家并未被平克的回应说服：他们的反应还需要那些对作品更为客观的评价。

批评

斯蒂芬·平克《人性中的善良天使：暴力为什么会减少》收到了各种各样的评论。[1] 澳大利亚伦理哲学家 * 彼得·辛格 * 称其为一部"极为重要的作品"，[2] 而美国政治学家罗伯特·杰维斯 * 认为平克发现的那些趋势"并非过于细微——很多变化都涉及一个量级或更多。即使他的解释并不令人信服，但也十分严谨，论证充分。"[3]

尽管许多学者同意平克的数据的确表明暴力在减少，但批评家们却不同意平克为此做出的解释。[4] 例如，美国学者布拉德利·A. 塞耶 * 认为暴力减少似乎更可能在于西方世界的权力制衡，比平克想象的情况更为脆弱。[5] 其他学者则认为，平克并未足够重视与文化因素相对的物质与制度因素[6]。

对平克持批评态度的学者可分为两类：第一类学者对书中的概念基础提出质疑，第二类学者则强调其数据存在缺陷。

第二类学者的质疑在方法论方面：死亡率数据是从哪里收集

的？怎样收集的？又为什么这样去阐释？美籍黎巴嫩统计学家纳西姆·尼古拉斯·塔勒布 * 指出平克的统计分析存在一些不合理推测，[7] 声称："他从以往数据得出的估计存在重大错误。根据前几年死亡人数的记录几乎不可能预测下一年可能死亡的人数，因此这样得出的下降趋势偏差很大。一个生物事件就能摧毁一个地区的人口。"[8] 澳大利亚学者杰夫·刘易斯 * 也批评平克依据的数据库实在太小，对战后死亡人数数据的排除也是有问题的。

> 斯蒂芬·平克《人性中的善良天使：暴力为什么会减少》是我读过的最重要的一本书——迄今为止，并非仅仅在今年……该书以暴力为主题，却描绘了一幅非凡的画面：在岁月长河的流淌中，世界逐步发展，相比以前暴力已经大大减少。就如何促进世界获取正面效应方面，它的确为人们提供了一个全新的视角。
>
> ——比尔·盖茨：《我的书架》

回应

对平克在《人性中的善良天使》中使用的概念方法提出质疑的批评家有英国的政治哲学家约翰·格雷 * 和美国记者伊丽莎白·科尔伯特 *。格雷指出，平克将自然科学与人文主义混为一体是错误的。参照 19 世纪自然主义者查尔斯·达尔文 *——进化科学 * 史与人文主义理性社会哲学史上的先驱人物——的遗留问题，格雷写道："更多时候，自然科学与人文主义间的矛盾往往比统一频繁得多。对于平克这样一位虔诚的达尔文主义者而言，认为由于某种世界观的传播，世界就变得更加和谐，简直太讽刺了。达尔文主义中根本没有什么能表明思想和信仰能改变人类生活。"[9]

同样，伊丽莎白·科尔伯特评论说，导致平克所谓道德进步的因素同样也导致了历史上最严重的暴行。

平克在回应以上批评时重申了自己的立场：[10] 他并未宣称世界已经比较安全，而是——从客观上讲——暴力已经减少。[11] 他认为塔勒布似乎误解了《人性中的善良天使》的整体设计：它只是描述性的，并非预测性的，[12] 另外，他也没有想方设法预测未来的暴力情况。[13] 因此，塔勒布所指出的问题与书中关于暴力为什么会减少的阐释并不相干。

针对像刘易斯这样的批评家，平克反驳道，他们只关注数据中的个别事例而忽略了全景。即使一些数据的确不精确，但全景图仍然能够表明暴力在减少。

目前以上争论尚未使平克对作品做出重大修改。但是，他们敦促平克回归其论点并拿出更多的数据予以支撑。

冲突与共识

尽管《人性中的善良天使》很受欢迎，但人们对于书中的主要论点很少达成一致，许多批评家对这些观点也并不信服。不过平克提供的暴力趋势的有关数据得到了较为广泛的认同。的确，来自人类安全报告项目＊的一份 2012 年的文件探讨了平克的作品并得出结论："今天学术界已达成广泛共识：国家之间的战争数量和致死性已极大下降。"[14]

平克并非指出几个世纪以来暴力已经减少的第一人。因此，到底是因为他才达成共识，还是因为历史学或犯罪学＊（探索、理解、预防个人及社会犯罪行为的研究领域）等领域已经达成这种共识，这一点还不够清楚。不管是哪种情况，平克都为人们呈现出了之前从未编辑过的数据。从这点而言，他为这一讨论贡献了原始的研究。

　　继巴黎恐怖主义分子袭击法国讽刺漫画杂志《查理周刊》*、叙利亚 * 持续不断的冲突之后，平克又回到自己的提案上。谈及人所共知的全球冷战 * 时期——1991 年以苏联的最终解体而结束，平克于 2015 年 9 月在英国《卫报》发表文章说道："我不断更新图表以审视我的乐观主义……令人沮丧的是，冷战之后内战数量急剧下降——从 1992 年的 26 起到 2007 年的 4 起——又在 2014 年反弹到 11 起……其中叙利亚战争，也导致全球死亡率在 60 年的巨幅下降后又小幅反弹……好消息是这不过是唯一的坏消息：每一种其他类型的暴力发生率已经跌至历史最低，甚至仍在继续下降。"[15]

---

1. 认知科学视角下的冲突、暴力、和平与正义（课程大纲）上有评论列表，登录日期 2015 年 12 月 30 日，http://web.stanford.edu/class/symsys203/。

2. 彼得·辛格："暴力是历史吗？"，《纽约时报》，2011 年 10 月 6 日，登录日期 2015 年 12 月 30 日，http://www.nytimes.com/2011/10/09/books/review/the-beter-angels-of-our-nature-by-steven-pinker-book-review。

3. 罗伯特·杰维斯："预言家平克"，《国家利益》，2011 年 11 月—12 月，登录日期 2015 年 12 月 30 日，http://nationalinterest.org/bookreview/pinker-the-prophet-6072。

4. 尼尔斯·佩特·格莱迪奇等："论坛：战争的消亡"，《国际研究评论》第 15 卷，2013 年第 3 期，第 396—419 页。

5. 布拉德利·阿尔弗雷德·塞耶："人类不是天使：质疑战争消亡的理由"，载"论坛：战争的消亡"，《国际研究评论》第 15 卷，2013 年第 3 期，第 407 页。

6. 杰克·S. 列维和威廉·R. 汤普森："战争的消亡：多元轨迹与扩散趋势"，载"论坛：战争的消亡"，《国际研究评论》第 15 卷，2013 年第 3 期，第 412 页。

7. 纳西姆·尼古拉斯·塔勒布："'长期和平'是统计假象"，登录日期 2015 年 12 月 30 日，http://www.fooledbyrandomness.com/longpeace.pdf。

8. 纳西姆·尼古拉斯·塔勒布，脸书，登录日期 2015 年 12 月 30 日，https://www.facebook.com/permalink.php?story_fbid=101516419318533758&id=13012333374。

9. 约翰·格雷："和平之幻灭"，《前景》，2011 年 9 月 21 日，登录日期 2015 年 12 月 30 日，http://www.prospectmagazine.co.uk/features/john-gray-steven-pinker-violence-review。

10. 了解此辩论，见约翰·格雷："约翰·格雷：关于暴力和战争，斯蒂芬·平克是错误的"，《卫报》，2015 年 3 月 13 日，登录日期 2015 年 12 月 30 日，http://www.theguardian.com/books/2015/mar/13/john-gray-steven-pinker-wrong-violence-war-declining。

11. 斯蒂芬·平克："就《人性中的善良天使：暴力为什么会减少》被频繁问及的问题"，登录日期 2015 年 12 月 30 日，http://stevenpinker.com/pages/frequently-asked-questions-about-better-angels-our-nature-why-violence-has-declined。

12. 斯蒂芬·平克："为好战所愚弄。针对纳西姆·塔勒布'长期和平是统计假象'的回应"，登录日期 2015 年 12 月 30 日，http://stevenpinker.com/files/comments_on_taleb_by_s_pinker.pdf。

13. 平克："为好战所愚弄"。

14. 人类安全报告项目，"全球暴力减少：现实还是神话？"，2014 年 3 月 3 日，登录日期 2015 年 12 月 29 日，http:/www.hsrgroup.org/docs/Publications/HSR2013/HSR_2013_Press_Release.pdf。

15. 斯蒂芬·平克："好消息：世界真的在改善"，《卫报》，2015 年 9 月 11 日，登录日期 2015 年 12 月 19 日，http://www.theguardian.com/commentisfree/2015/sep/11/news-isis-syria-headlines-violence-steven-pinker。

10 后续争议

要点 ⚷—

- 《人性中的善良天使》为暴力正在减少的命题提供了目前最为全面的数据支持。

- 尽管我们不能说因《人性中的善良天使》催生了某一"思想流派"，很多思想家和公众人物已经受到了该书的影响与启发。

- 该书不仅影响了学术界的人士，也影响了一些企业家，如美国微软的创始人比尔·盖茨，脸书的创始人马克·扎克伯格。

应用与问题

斯蒂芬·平克《人性中的善良天使：暴力为什么会减少》出版于 2011 年，因此追踪该书对其他作家的影响为时尚早。不过，我们可以从该书出版以来人们对它的应用来评估一下其影响力。一些关于暴力趋向的研究引用了该书的内容。[1] 同行评议期刊《进化心理学》2014 年专刊聚焦暴力演变问题，并多处引用《人性中的善良天使》[2]。在社会科学的众多学科中，读者也对《人性中的善良天使》做出了回应，或修改，或完善，或批评其中的一些缺陷。

比如，2015 年出版的一本书中，研究犯罪历史的历史学家和社会学家对 1950 年以来 55 个国家凶杀案的下降进行了评估，发现暴力下降趋势已经非常普遍。[3] 他们的论文以平克的作品为参考文献，但与《人性中的善良天使》的主张相反的是，他们并没有发现暴力减少和现代化*进程（人类社会从前工业时代、传统时期、农业时期和宗教时期完全转向工业化、城市化和世俗化的过程）之间有密切联系。尽管上述 55 个国家都有暴力减少的迹象，但只有富裕的、西方民主体制的国家才体现出这种联系。他们非常谦逊地对平克的论题予以总结："认为暴力犯罪减少是因为现代化进程在改变世界……这是一个极其宽泛的命题。我们的研究仅限于一种单一暴力形式，只有 60 年时间跨度，样本也并不随机，主要选择富裕的西方民主体制国家。由于经过这样的精挑细选，高度现代化并未提供充分的解释，不过这一观点相比有争议的观点而言，与相关数据更为契合。"[4]

> 2012 年 4 月，我们邀请几十位美国范围内的学者在密歇根罗切斯特奥克兰大学参加为期一天的会议，主题为"暴力之进化"。会议前一天，大家刚好参加了平克对其新书《人性中的善良天使：暴力为什么会减少》所做的讲座。我们当时按照分组讨论的方式邀请了许多不同领域研究暴力的顶尖学者，有心理学的、犯罪学的、生物学的、人类学的、考古学的、法学的、哲学的以及医学的。
>
> ——托德·K. 沙克尔福德 *，拉纳尔德·D. 汉森 *：
> 《暴力进化之前言》

思想流派

说《人性中的善良天使》仍然尚未创建一个思想流派主要有两个原因：一是因为该书才出版不久，现在谈论其长期影响还为时过早；二是该书涵盖范围广泛，包含众多学科。因此，它也许会对明确认同书中观点的人产生影响，却尚未催生出一个有凝聚力的团体。

《人性中的善良天使》在通常的世界观中占有一席之地，这种世界观可以广义地界定为对人性进步持乐观态度。据平克所言，持有同样观点的思想家和哲学家有法国哲学家奥古斯特·孔德*，英国哲学家约翰·斯图亚特·穆勒*、托马斯·霍布斯*、约翰·洛克*，苏格兰经济学家大卫·休谟*，以及德国哲学家伊曼努尔·康德*。该书还吸引了学术圈内外不同领域的众多思想家。美国技术专家和慈善家比尔·盖茨、马克·扎克伯格和知名学者澳大利亚哲学家彼得·辛格*、英国政治学家*亚当·罗伯茨*都称赞这本书。5辛格曾称它是一本"极其重要的著作"。6对他们而言，该书为历史真正的进步（也许在辛格的案例中是一种道德进步）带来了希望。

当代研究

到目前为止，还没有人明确继承《人性中的善良天使》中提出的整体规划。但有很多研究者均以此书为出发点展开其科学研究。几位人类学*领域的研究者正在调查暴力的生物起源和文化起源。他们要么采用更多细节阐释延伸平克书中的观点，要么将其看作一个反面的出发点。例如，一些人已经接受他的观点，赞同暴力会随着人们从狩猎社会进入依照国家路线建立的社会而减少。7另一些人则持相反观点，他们认为狩猎社会并不比国家社会更加暴力。8他们也像平克一样，以数据和已收集的证据来证实自己的观点。

另外，进化心理学*也是当前学术研究中采用《人性中的善良天使》做参考的例子。该书在这一领域引发了关于暴力生物起源的争论，因此暴力进化研究特刊的编辑对此书深表感谢。9最后要讲的事例是，国际政治学领域也参照《人性中的善良天使》进行学术讨论。2013年，同行评议杂志《国际研究评论》刊载的一篇文章说："几位作者声称近几十年来'战争在减少'（其中一位认知心理学家用洋洋洒洒 800 页的巨著进行了论述（平克，2011））。"文章继续写道："尽管这是一部宏篇巨制，但并不意味着争论的结束，而是一场长期讨论的开始。"[10]

1. 蒂莫西·科勒等："人性中的善良天使：普韦部落西南部前西班牙农民中的暴力在减少"，《美国考古》第 79 卷，2014 年第 3 期，第 444—464 页。
2. 托德·肯尼迪·沙克尔福德和拉纳尔德·汉森：《暴力演进》，纽约：斯普林格出版社，2014 年。
3. 加里·拉弗里等："'善良天使'如何发挥作用？1950 年以来国家层面凶杀案下降趋势评估"，《欧洲犯罪学》第 4 期第 12 卷，2015 年，第 482—504 页。
4. 拉弗里等："'善良天使'如何发挥作用？"，第 495 页。
5. 亚当·罗伯茨："长期和平越发长久"，《生存》第 54 卷，2012 年第 1 期，第 175—183 页。
6. 彼得·辛格："暴力是历史吗？"，《纽约时报》，2011 年 10 月 6 日，登录日期 2015 年 12 月 30 日，http://www.nytimes.com/2011/10/09/books/review/the-better-angels-of-our-nature-by-steven-pinker-book-review.html。
7. Nam C. Kim："天使，幻觉，祸患，及妄想：暴力与人类"，《人类学评论》第 41 卷，2012 年第 4 期，第 239—272 页。
8. 杰弗里·本杰明等："暴力：发现和平"，《科学》第 338 卷，2012 年第 6105 期，第 327 页。
9. 沙克尔福德和汉森：《暴力演进》。
10. 尼尔斯·佩特·格莱迪奇等："论坛：战争的消亡"，《国际研究评论》第 15 卷，2013 年第 3 期，第 396—419 页。

11 当代印迹

要点 &—

- 《人性中的善良天使》仍然是暴力史和暴力起源争论的焦点。

- 平克的这本著作一直在挑战大众业已接受的观点：当今时代是人类历史上最为暴力的时代。

- 对该作品持批评态度的评论家，普遍对人性及其未来持有消极的世界观。

地位

平克的著作《人性中的善良天使：暴力为什么会减少》为其乐观的思想——在历史发展进程中，暴力在稳定减少——进行了辩护。书中的核心论点仍然为人们讨论和引用。比如，新近出版的关于道德和同理心的研究作品就引用了平克的相关思想。[1]另外，这些思想还被用来探究新的地域、不同历史时期暴力的发展趋势，[2]在目前暴力争论中也仍在被引用。[3]

该书对关于暴力与气候变化*间关系的持续争论有所促进。平克提及了全球变暖*，但却指出全球变暖对暴力层面并没有十分重要的影响。他认为，冲突更容易在贫穷、政治不稳定的国家出现，而不是在遭受自然灾害的国家，"既然环境问题至多是更依赖政治、社会组织的混合物中的因素之一，资源战争就不是不可避免的，即使是在气候变化的世界。"[4]对此，平克解释说，高度民主和富裕的国家能对自然灾害做出迅速反应并控制其后果，这就帮助他们避免了这些事件可能引发的暴力后果。

《人性中的善良天使》激发了人们对暴力趋势进行统计研究的兴趣，以及对引发暴力（或限制暴力）的相关因素展开研究的兴趣。目前已达成的一致是，《人性中的善良天使》是关于这些问题所有讨论的重要参考书目。不过现在说这一趋势是否会持续下去还为时过早。

> 《人性中的善良天使》是一部极其重要的著作。但未来会怎样呢？我们对暴力认识的提升，就像平克在其著作中说的那样，能成为维护和平、减少暴力的重要工具，但其他因素仍然在发挥作用。
>
> ——彼得·辛格：《暴力是历史吗？》

互动

《人性中的善良天使》借用了不同学科的研究目的和方法，是一部跨学科作品。平克的灵感部分来源于他的挑战欲，他想挑战社会学*领域普遍存在的观点——人类生来是一块白板。赞同这一观点的人认为，人类没有什么天生的生物或心理*机能：一切均源于社会和文化（平克认为，这是颇具影响力的美籍德裔人类学家*法兰兹·博厄斯*的追随者们所持的观点）。[5] 如果真是这样，暴力就不可能是一个生物现象，而仅仅是社会和文化现象。平克对这一观点提出质疑，指出人类天生具有某种暴力倾向；这些暴力倾向，在某种程度上而言，是可能在历史发展进程中被驯化的。

《人性中的善良天使》也对暴力正在增加这一观点提出质疑。这些质疑立刻引发回应：例如，英国哲学家约翰·格雷*就平克关于人性和历史的根本概念做出回应。格雷的世界观是霍布斯主义的，即对人性持消极、悲观的态度。17世纪英国哲学家托马斯·霍布斯指出人类是自私、自利的，如果没有强有力的政府抑制这样的冲动，我们会永远生活在冲突当中。格雷关于人性及其未来走向的观点与平克完全不同。因此，他们对于人类暴力问题存在分歧也就不足为奇。

持续争议

平克与其反对者之间的辩论更多在于思想、世界观和人性概念的不同，而不是在平克的作品上。这些争论很难有结果。写《人性中的善良天使》的过程中，平克对几个思想流派提出了反对意见。其中一个是人类学派，平克将其称为"维护和平的人类学家"。他认为，这一学派受议题驱动，只想证明非国家＊社会是和平的。相比之下，平克并未想证明人类天生是善良的或者暴力的。他描绘了一幅细致入微的图景：人类可以是平和的也可以是暴力的，主要取决于他们的生存环境。不过，他的论述提及非常关键的一点：以国家为基础的社会有助于减少暴力。这些人类学家回应平克说，他们的目标不是意识形态＊研究，而是实证＊研究。[6]

还有一个难有定论的争论发生在平克与格雷之间。他认为平克对未来的想象是由于其对科学的盲目信仰和对人性更深刻认识的缺乏。格雷本人的观点是"和平、自由与战争、暴政交替出现……文明不会变得更加普遍、更有影响力，它仍然是本质脆弱的，会不断屈服于野蛮。"[7]平克回应说，他们之间存在意识形态方面的分歧："作为他（格雷）反对理性、科学与启蒙人文主义运动的一部分，他坚持认为几个世纪以来人类的抗争并没有使我们过得更好。"[8]平克强调了他的统计数据能够说明暴力在减少，以此对格雷挑战做出回应。

1. 让·德赛迪和杰森·考威尔："道德与同理心之间的复杂关系",《认知科学发展趋势》第 18 卷, 2014 年第 7 期, 第 337—339 页。

2. 蒂莫西·科勒等："人性中的善良天使: 普韦部落西南部前西班牙农民中的暴力在减少",《美国考古》第 79 卷, 2014 年第 3 期, 第 444—464 页。

3. 斯蒂芬·平克："好消息: 世界真的在改善",《卫报》, 2015 年 11 月 9 日, 登录日期 2015 年 12 月 19 日, http://www.theguardian.com/commentisfree/2015/sep/11/news-isis-syria-headlines-violence-steven-pinker。

4. 斯蒂芬·平克:《人性中的善良天使: 暴力为什么会减少》, 伦敦: 企鹅图书, 2011 年, 第 377 页。

5. 斯蒂芬·平克:《白板: 人性的现代否定》, 伦敦: 企鹅图书, 2002 年, 第 36 页。

6. 杰弗里·本杰明等："暴力: 发现和平",《科学》第 338 卷, 2012 年第 6105 期, 第 327 页。

7. 约翰·格雷："约翰·格雷: 关于暴力和战争, 斯蒂芬·平克是错误的",《卫报》, 2015 年 3 月 13 日, 登录日期 2015 年 12 月 30 日, http://www.theguardian.com/books/2015/mar/13/john-gray-steven-pinker-wrong-violence-war-declining。

8. 斯蒂芬·平克："猜猜怎么样了？只要看看数据就知道更多人的生活在和平之中",《卫报》, 2015 年 3 月 20 日, 登录日期 2015 年 12 月 30 日, http://www.theguardian.com/commentisfree/2015/mar/20/wars-john-gray-conflict-peace。

12 未来展望

要点 🗝

- 《人性中的善良天使》可能仍会是未来暴力研究中的参考点。
- 它很可能对暴力史和暴力心理学＊之间联系的研究产生影响。
- 《人性中的善良天使》也可能对发展心理学＊（关于婴儿思想及其从出生到成年心理机能如何发展的研究）领域产生影响。平克建议研究暴力演变应通过观察一个人的成长环境。

潜力

　　斯蒂芬·平克《人性中的善良天使：暴力为什么会减少》很可能成为未来历史学、社会学＊、暴力心理学相关争论的核心。因为它的确提出了一个关于暴力的大胆命题，并为之提供了明确的方法论。

　　平克的数据表明暴力正在减少。该书的一大优势在于书中论点是建立在证据基础之上的。但是，有可能会出现新的数据证明暴力在增加，从而与平克的观点相矛盾。平克在 2015 年 9 月 11 日发表的一篇文章中谈到了新趋势，声称这些新趋势仍然支持他的命题："人类这一可怜的物种所能想到的最集中的毁灭方式就是世界大战与核战争，因此我们努力了 70 年去避免这些战争。而同样极具破坏力的大国之间的战争也已经消失大概 62 年之久了。"[1]

　　该书整体上采用描述性方法，向人们展示了暴力发展的历史趋势，并对暴力进行了心理学阐释。尽管平克并未尝试对暴力如何得以控制和减少展开说明，但他所牵出的心理学与社会之间的关系在整个论述中发挥着重要作用。这些思想也许会对教育领域产生特殊影响，影响人们教授和平与合作的方式。

> 新闻提要真是对历史的误导。人们对危险的感知被记忆中的事例扭曲——这就是为什么我们更害怕被鲸鱼吃掉而不是从楼梯上滚落下来，其实后者更容易导致我们死亡。无论和平的领土有多么宽广，仍然不会让新闻和人类忘记最近的战争和暴行。
>
> ——斯蒂芬·平克："好消息：世界真的在改善"

未来方向

尽管《人性中的善良天使》旨在将心理学和历史联系起来，但该书探讨心理学的篇幅明显短于平克对暴力史的回顾。显然，需要做更多的研究来发现历史语境如何塑造心理状态。平克提到认知人类学＊中的一个模型，该模型指出建立和理解社会关系的方法是普遍的，这就是美国人类学家艾伦·费斯克＊创立的"关系模型"。但是认知人类学、心理学和社会之间如何联系的细节还并不清楚。因此，就冲突与合作的演进方面还需要做大量研究，这也会使该书的阐释部分更具实质性基础。

《人性中的善良天使》一书为兴趣在暴力起源方面的进化心理学家＊和发展心理学家提供了研究起点。对该书核心命题感兴趣的社会学家和历史学家很可能会对其基本数据展开研究，认真分析历史走向从而肯定或反驳该命题。

平克的思想还可能在技术领域得到应用。美国脸书创始人马克·扎克伯格＊曾问平克，是否有数据说明因特网在减少暴力方面也发挥一定作用。平克回答，新技术发挥着传播世界大同主义＊

（认为所有人类属于一个共同体）的作用，而世界大同主义对暴力拥有积极的影响。[2]

也许平克还没拥有一批追随者或学生对《人性中的善良天使》中所提出的命题继续展开研究，但他身边有很多同事持有赞同态度，如澳大利亚哲学家彼得·辛格*、英国进化心理学家理查德·道金斯*。他们可能会持续思考书中提出的那些问题。

小结

暴力是人类历史和心理学的一个核心特征。《人性中的善良天使》通过对暴力史及其心理根源的综合研究将二者结合起来。这本宏篇巨制是平克诸多畅销书中的一本，也是在学术界和更广泛领域引发最热烈争论的一本书。这些争论可能会一直持续下去。

先前的暴力研究或者关注暴力史、或者关注暴力行为背后的心理状态，几乎没有人将二者结合起来。此外，大多数暴力研究倾向于以极端的方式界定人性：要么人性本善，受到社会扭曲而变得暴力；要么人性本恶，根本无法为社会所改变。《人性中的善良天使》并未以上述两种观点中的任何一种为基础。平克设法阐释先天与后天之间如何相互作用：尽管人类生物学在很多方面都无法改变，但社会与文化的确能对我们的行为产生影响。

《人性中的善良天使》是十分具有吸引力的一本书，因为它对人性的未来充满乐观态度。该书的论点以数据和统计分析为支撑，并非天真的乐观主义。该书也极具挑战性，因为其乐观主义与很多人认为世界日益危险、充满威胁的直觉观点形成对比。它之所以拥有如此突出的地位，部分原因是它能引发人们就人性中最核心的方面之一——暴力——展开激烈讨论。

1. 斯蒂芬·平克："好消息：世界真的在改善"，《卫报》，2015年9月11日，登录日期 2015 年 12 月 30 日，http://www.the guardian.com/commentisfree/2015/sep/11/news-isis-syria-headlines-violence-steven-pinker。

2. 马克·扎克伯格："年度好书"，脸书，2015年1月28日，登录日期 2015 年 12 月 30 日，https://www.facebook.com/ayearofbooks/posts/831583243554273。

术语表

1. **无政府主义**：政治哲学理论，提倡消除国家，建立自制、自由的社会。无政府主义有很多分支，但他们的共同特征是拒绝制度化的政治权力。其中主要代表人物是俄国革命家米哈伊尔·巴枯宁。

2. **人类学**：研究人类的学科，涉及人性各个方面的研究，如：生理、语言、社会、文化等方面，属于社会科学领域。

3. **考古学**：通过研究古代器物、建筑物、人文景观（自然与人工造物的结合）来研究过去人类生活和活动的学科，属于社会科学领域。

4. **无神论**：主张没有神灵。

5. **生物学**：自然科学的一个领域，主要研究生物体的发育、结构、功能、分类以及分布。

6. **《查理周刊》袭击案**：2015 年 1 月 7 日，两名自称也门基地组织成员的持枪者对法国讽刺周刊《查理周刊》发起的袭击案件，杂志社多名员工受伤或死亡。

7. **基督教**：亚布拉罕一神论宗教，其教义的主要文本为《新约》，核心信仰为耶稣是弥撒亚、人类的救世主，是《旧约》中的预言之说。

8. **文明化进程**：斯蒂芬·平克从生于德国的社会学家诺伯特·埃利亚斯处借用的一个术语。该术语用以说明中世纪开始的制度变化对人类心理产生了一定影响，有助于减少人类暴力。

9. **气候变化**：天气模式的长期变化。气候变化大多数情况下根据考古证据、气温测量以及动植物的出现情况予以测定。

10. **认知**：狭义上而言，认知指感知之后予以处理的思维机能，如记忆、判断、决策以及语言。广义上而言，认知指全部思维过

程，包括认知、记忆、注意力、语言、决策、推理、判断以及解决问题。

11. **认知人类学**：使用认知科学的目的与方法来研究人类学的一种途径。

12. **认知科学**：吸收哲学、心理学、神经科学、人工智能、语言学以及人类学研究成果对思维和大脑进行的跨学科研究。其核心假设是思维和大脑都是计算代表性装置，在某些方面类似于计算机，因此我们可以通过试验的方法对其进行研究。

13. **冷战**：1947—1991 年间西方阵营（美国及其联盟）与东方阵营（苏联及其联盟）之间的政治、军事对峙阶段。之所以称之为"冷"，是因为它从未引发美国与苏联之间的直接冲突，而是由卫星国展开，主要涉及权力的相对分配。

14. **集体无政府主义**：一种政治理论，主张废除国家，生产资料和生产工具都应归集体所有。

15. **殖民主义**：一个地区的强权对另一地区的统治与剥削。

16. **世界大同主义**：信奉所有人类是同一个共同体的公民。根据斯蒂芬·平克的观点，世界大同主义是有助于减少暴力的一种文化力量。

17. **犯罪学**：探索、认识、预防个人及社会犯罪行为的跨学科研究领域。

18. **十字军东征**：11 世纪至 13 世纪期间发生的一系列战争。第一次十字军东征发生于 1095 年，西欧基督教军队对战穆斯林军事力量，收复圣地（约旦河与地中海之间的区域）。

19. **达尔文主义**：与英国自然主义者查尔斯·达尔文及其进化论相关的一系列思想。

20. **民主**：人民自由选举其代表的一种政治体制。

21. **发展心理学**：研究婴儿思维及其从出生到成年心理机能发展过程的学科。

22. **家庭暴力**：家庭环境中通常由伴侣实施的肢体和心理暴力。

23. **经济学**：研究经济制度——商品生产、交易与消费（物质或非物质的，如服务）——的学科。

24. **同理心**：从他者角度而不是自身角度来理解其处境、经历与情感的能力。

25. **实证的**：该术语用以形容通过观察或实验、而非仅仅通过思考或理论化得出的知识。

26. **经验主义**：哲学思想流派之一，认为知识源于经验而非天生。相关哲学家有约翰·洛克、大卫·休谟、托马斯·霍布斯。心理学界也有这一分支。

27. **启蒙运动**：18 世纪欧洲出现的文化运动（美国也有一部分），其特征是追求理性、捍卫自由、包容与权利。

28. **公平女性主义**：公平女性主义者主要要求法律上的权利平等（如干同样的工作，女性应该获得和男性同等的工资），但在性别角色上保持中立。性别女权主义者则有更宽广的视野，通常认为性别角色是一种社会建构。

29. **人种学**：通过观察民族内部对民族文化进行研究的学科。

30. **欧元区**：欧盟 19 个成员国之间形成的货币联盟（欧盟总共有 28 个成员国，其中 9 个成员国并未加入欧元区）。这些国家均使用欧元作为他们的通用货币。

31. **进化**：一个既定生物种群的遗传特征随着时间在不同代系发生变化的过程。

32. **进化心理学**：从现代进化理论视角对人类与非人类心理进行研究的学科。

33. **扩展圈**：澳大利亚道德哲学家彼得·辛格提出的一个概念。辛格指出，当我们的道德关怀延伸到和我们并不亲近的生命时，那就是

一种道德进步。这与平克将同理心作为减少暴力的一种心理机能有一定联系。

34. **实验心理学**：通过可量可测结果的方法对人类思维和行为进行研究的学科，具有一定的精确度。

35. **女性主义**：以为女性争取平等权利为目标的运动。广义上来说，就是在社会、政治文化方面拥护女性的运动。

36. **性别**：与男性、女性差异广泛相关的一组特征，性别差异并不像两性差异一样只是生理方面的。

37. **种族灭绝**：基于种族、民族、宗教、文化、民族特征对一个族群实施的系统灭绝。

38. **全球变暖**：由于人类对气候和环境的影响，地球平均温度逐渐升高的现象。

39. **人文主义**：人性至上而非宗教或"神学"机构与人物至上的一系列理性准则。

40. **人权**：仅仅因为是人类而获得的最基本的一套权利，如：免受酷刑。

41. **人类安全报告项目**：研究和平与冲突的一项计划，总部在加拿大，旨在检验暴力冲突的长期发展趋势。

42. **狩猎采集者**：通过狩猎、采集而不是靠发展农业生存的人类。

43. **意识形态**：群体或个人所秉持的规范、信仰及理论系统。

44. **宗教法庭**：13 世纪基督教会为确保信仰与宗教仪式的纯洁性所设立的一个机构，后因在排除异教徒时使用酷刑而臭名昭著。

45. **利维坦**：《旧约》中的一只神秘怪兽。该表述被英国哲学家托马斯·霍布斯用以指代一种绝对的主权。

46. **语言学**：研究语言及其不同方面的学科。

47. **中世纪的**：与中世纪相关的（5 到 15 世纪）。

48. **中世纪**：5 世纪（西罗马帝国衰落）到 15 世纪（欧洲文艺复兴时期开始）的一段欧洲历史时期。

49. **现代化**：社会从前工业时期、传统时期、农耕时期、宗教时期转型到完全工业化、城市化和世俗化时期的过程。

50. **道德哲学**：研究"正确行为"之本质及伦理的学科。

51. **先天论者**：心理学语境下，先天论者认为人类思维中的某些东西是"天生的"——换言之，我们生来有之。

52. **先天与后天**：影响成长的两种相对因素："先天"指天生的生理因素，而"后天"指外在的环境因素（包括文化和社会因素）。

53. **纳粹主义**：20 世纪三四十年代德国纳粹党的政治意识形态思想。

54. **高贵的野蛮人**：指假设存在的、尚未被文明腐蚀和扭曲的原生态人。该术语来自德莱顿剧作《征服格拉纳达》（1672），通常和卢梭的理论联系使用："自然状态"或自然的人类状态是和平的。

55. **非国家社会**：没有稳定国家或权威的社会，例如群体、部落或酋邦。这些社会在史前期（约公元前 1 万年）广泛存在，现在只是一种边缘化的生活方式。

56. **规范的**：符合指导行为的规范与规则的。

57. **和平主义**：拒绝战争、暴力和军国主义。

58. **哲学**：对现实本质最基本的系统研究。

59. **政策分析 / 分析师**：研究、评估政策、计划及它们的可能影响，旨在解决公众问题；政策分析师就是从事这一研究的人。

60. **政治学**：从多维视角研究政治、政府或政治制度如何运作的学科。

61. **规定性的**：与旨在加强某类行为的准则、规则相关的。

62. **心理学**：对群体或个人思想和行为的科学研究。心理学研究思维如何运作，比如感知、记忆、决策、工作。该学科属于社会科学领域。一般而言，"心理学"和"心理学的"这两个术语均用来指思维的工作方式。

63. **好战**：喜欢挑衅或好斗的倾向。

64. **科学方法**：科学中研究世界所使用的一系列步骤，包括谨慎构想假设并检验该假设的方法。

65. **世俗的**：与宗教无关的，不受宗教规则约束的。

66. **社会学**：研究社会的学科，社会科学的领域之一。社会学家们研究的主题一般有宗教、政治和社会阶级等。

67. **社会科学**：包括人类学、考古学、人口学、经济学、历史学、人文地理学、国际关系学、法学、语言学、政治学、教育学以及心理学的广泛的学术研究领域。

68. **自然状态**：政治哲学中的一个概念，指假想中社会与国家出现之前人们的生活状态。

69. **叙利亚冲突**：2011 年以来叙利亚持续不断的纷争，以反对叙利亚总统巴沙尔·阿萨德政府的示威游行为开端，抗议者要求总统辞职。至今冲突仍未停止。

70. **恐怖主义**：旨在引发恐慌的行为，通常是为了产生政治影响。

71. **睾丸素**：人类与非人类动物中均会出现的一种荷尔蒙，大多数情况下，由人类男性的睾丸分泌而成，少数情况下，由人类女性的卵巢分泌而成，通常与男性特征相关。

72. **乌克兰冲突**：2013 年开始，乌克兰顿涅茨克亲俄、反俄派之间的持续冲突。顿涅茨克是乌克兰的一个地区，该地区大部分居民都说俄语。

73. **乌普萨拉冲突数据计划**：20 世纪 70 年代由瑞典乌普萨拉大学主持的一项计划，旨在收集世界范围内暴力冲突的相关数据。

74. **女性权利**：针对促进女性与男性平等的权利。

75. **世界大战**：世界上大多数国家参与的战争。该术语用以指 20 世纪的两大事件：第一次世界大战（1914—1918）和第二次世界大战（1939—1945）。

人名表

1. 米哈伊尔·巴枯宁（1814—1876），俄国革命思想家，作为无政府主义运动的创立者之一而享有盛名。

2. 法兰兹·博厄斯（1858—1942），美籍德裔思想家，现代人类学的先驱之一，曾在哥伦比亚大学自己创建的学院内任教，主要代表作之一是1911年出版的《原始人的思维》。

3. 诺姆·乔姆斯基（1928年生），美国语言学家、认知科学家与政治活动家，麻省理工学院名誉教授，因生成语法理论而闻名。斯蒂芬·平克曾帮助将其语言思想介绍给广大民众。

4. 格雷戈里·克拉克（1957年生），经济史学家，专业研究国家财富。

5. 罗杰·科恩（1955年生），英国记者，《纽约时报》和《国际纽约时报》的专栏作家。

6. 奥古斯特·孔德（1798—1857），法国哲学家，实证主义（哲学运动，以所有知识都是模仿科学知识范例的思想为基础）的创始人之一，也被视为社会学的创始人之一。

7. 勒达·科斯米德斯（1957年生），美国心理学家，以进化心理学的创始人之一而著称。

8. 约翰·克劳福（1783—1868），苏格兰外交官，致力于民族学研究。

9. 马丁·戴利（1944年生），加拿大进化心理学家。

10. 查尔斯·达尔文（1809—1882），英国自然主义者，因其进化论的开创性著作《物种起源》（1859）而闻名。

11. 理查德·道金斯（1941年生），英国动物行为学家（研究动物行为的人）、进化心理学家，现任牛津大学新学院名誉研究员。因1976年出版的《自私的基因》而闻名，该书提出了以基因为中心的进化理论。

12. **大卫·多伊奇**（1953 年生），英国牛津大学物理学家，撰写过有关知识创造性和知识历史的文章。

13. **贾德·戴蒙**（1937 年生），美国加利福尼亚大学科学家、地理学教授，从事人类学、进化生物学及其他领域的研究。

14. **诺伯特·埃利亚斯**（1897—1990），德裔英国社会学家，《文明化进程》（1939 年在德国出版，1969 年译为英语）的作者。该书研究了行为方式如何随着时间而演变，以及这些演变对人类心理产生了怎样的影响。

15. **艾伦·费斯克**（1947 年生），美国加利福尼亚大学人类学家，从事人类学及人类关系心理学研究，因其"社会关系模型"理论而闻名。

16. **比尔·盖茨**（1955 年生），美国企业家、计算机程序师、慈善家，以微软公司创立者的身份而闻名。

17. **约书亚·戈尔茨坦**（1952 年生），美国华盛顿大学国际关系荣誉教授，专门研究战争与社会。

18. **丽贝卡·戈尔茨坦**（1950 年生），美国小说家，因小说《身心问题》而闻名，是斯蒂芬·平克的第三任妻子。

19. **约翰·格雷**（1948 年生），英国政治哲学家，《卫报》和《泰晤士报文学副刊》等报刊的长期撰稿人。最为著名的作品是《稻草狗：关于人类和其他动物的思考》（2003）、《黑色弥撒：世界末日的宗教和乌托邦的死亡》（2007），书中表达了对人性的悲观态度。

20. **泰德·罗伯特·古尔**（1936 年生），美国政治学家，研究政治冲突问题，现任马里兰大学荣誉教授。

21. **拉纳尔德·汉森**（2014 年逝世），奥克兰大学心理学教授，专门研究暴力与性倾向的进化心理学。

22. **托马斯·霍布斯**（1588—1679），研究不同主题的英国哲学家，但因其政治哲学而闻名，代表作是《利维坦》（1651）。

23. **大卫·休谟**（1711—1776），苏格兰哲学家，经验主义与怀疑论的代表人物之一，代表作是《人性论》。

24. **罗伯特·杰维斯**（1940年生），哥伦比亚大学国际事务学教授。

25. **伊曼努尔·康德**（1724—1804），德国哲学家，研究知识的各个领域。他的三"批判"作品是哲学史上最重要的著作。

26. **伊丽莎白·科尔伯特**（1961年生），美国记者，《纽约客》的撰稿人。

27. **斯蒂芬·科斯林**（1948年生），美国心理学家、神经科学家，因心理意象和信息处理方面的著作而闻名，是斯蒂芬·平克在哈佛大学的导师。

28. **杰夫·刘易斯**，澳大利亚皇家墨尔本理工大学媒体与文化研究教授，已发表有影响力的暴力与恐怖主义著作。

29. **亚伯拉罕·林肯**（1809—1865），美国第16任总统，于美国内战期间执政，战争刚刚结束就遭遇暗杀身亡。

30. **约翰·洛克**（1632—1704），英国经验主义哲学家，以思想概念和政治哲学而闻名。

31. **约翰·斯图亚特·穆勒**（1806—1873），英国哲学家、经济学家、政治思想家、功利主义的主要代表人物之一。代表作是《论自由》与《功利主义》。

32. **罗伯特·穆切布尔德**（1944年生），法国历史学家，专门研究暴力史。他也对性别史感兴趣。2011年，其著作《中世纪晚期到今天的暴力史》英译本问世。

33. **刘易斯·弗雷·理查森**（1881—1953），英国数学家，因气象学著作而闻名。他是首批采用数学及统计方法研究战争与冲突起因的思想家之一。

34. **亚当·罗伯茨**（1940年生），英国人，牛津大学国际关系学教授，因国际安全、国际组织、国际法学和公民抵抗的相关著作而闻名。

35. **让·雅克·卢梭**（1712—1778），法国哲学家、启蒙运动思想家，因政治哲学、人类本性和教育方面的著作而闻名。

36. **鲁道夫·拉梅尔**（1932—2014），暴力史学家，专门研究种族灭绝。他创造了术语"大规模屠杀"用以表示由政府武装力量实施的系统屠杀。

37. **托德·肯尼迪·沙克尔福德**（1971年生），美国进化心理学家，奥克兰大学教授。

38. **彼得·辛格**（1946年生），出生于澳大利亚的哲学家，普林斯顿大学生物伦理学教授，专门研究道德哲学、伦理学，因动物权利的相关著作而闻名。

39. **纳西姆·尼古拉斯·塔勒布**（1960年生），黎巴嫩裔美国统计学家，专门研究随机性和概率，代表作是《黑天鹅》。

40. **布拉德利·阿尔弗莱德·塞耶**，明尼苏达州德卢斯大学政治学副教授。撰写了《达尔文与国际关系：论战争与种族冲突的进化起源》（2004）一书。

41. **约翰·图比**（1952年生），美国人类学家，与妻子勒达·科斯米德斯一起以进化心理学著作而闻名。

42. **马戈·威尔逊**（1942—2009），加拿大进化心理学家，因凶杀及暴力风险的相关著作而闻名。

43. **马克·扎克伯格**（1984年生），美国因特网企业家，作为脸书创始人而闻名。

WAYS IN TO THE TEXT

KEY POINTS

- Born in 1954, Steven Pinker is a Canadian American professor of experimental psychology* at Harvard University and the author of many scholarly and popular books about language and human psychology. Experimental psychology is the study of the human mind and behavior in a way that is measurable and has a degree of scientific accuracy.

- *The Better Angels* argues that violence has declined over the course of human history, and explores the potential causes of that decline.

- Since its publication in 2011, *The Better Angels* has been widely regarded as one of the most controversial books about the history and psychology of violence.

Who Is Steven Pinker?

Steven Arthur Pinker, the author of *The Better Angels of Our Nature: Why Violence Has Declined* (2011), was born in Montréal, Canada, to Jewish parents in 1954. As a teenager he was, he says, "a true believer in Bakunin's anarchism."*[1] Mikhail Bakunin* was a Russian revolutionary and the founder of collectivist anarchism: * a political theory that argued for the abolition of the state, and for the tools and resources required for production to be collectively owned. But Pinker's antipathy towards the state ended in October 1969, when he was 15, as a result of a police strike in Montréal. The police were protesting against the fact that their counterparts in Toronto, another Canadian city, were paid more than them. The events of the next day began Pinker's reflections about violence in society: "When law enforcement vanishes, all manner of violence breaks out ... By 11 : 20 a.m. the first bank was robbed ... This decisive empirical* test left my politics in tatters (and offered a foretaste of a life as a scientist)."² (An empirical test is a test founded on observable evidence rather than theory.)

Steven Pinker went on to study psychology* (the science of the human mind and its role in behavior) as an undergraduate at Dawson College, an institution in Montreal. He earned a master's degree in Canada at McGill University before completing a doctorate in experimental psychology at Harvard University in the United States. He now works at Harvard as the Johnstone Family Professor in the psychology department. Pinker's initial area of interest, however, was not the psychology of violence, but linguistics* — the study of language, in all its various aspects. His first book, *The Language Instinct*, was published in 1994. In it he defends the ideas of the American linguist Noam Chomsky,* who argues that all humans are "hardwired" with the same language-learning structural approach to language: in other words, we are not born as "blank states." In other books Pinker has explored human psychology and how our psychological functions have evolved. These interests are evident in *The Better Angels.*

What Does *The Better Angels of Our Nature* Say?

In *The Better Angels* Steven Pinker states that human violence has declined over time. Though many assume that the world became more violent over the twentieth century, he argues the opposite. There is, he suggests, only an *impression* that violence is rising and that the future will bring even more violence. This impression is the result of our tendency to remember things that are easy to recall. We find it easier to remember shocking events that frighten us than events that seem more commonplace. In a feature written for the British *Guardian* newspaper in September 2015, Pinker says that this "is why we are more afraid of getting eaten by a shark than falling down the stairs, though the latter is more likely to kill us."[3] He argues that this tendency is exploited by a media that delights in showing violent events. As a result, we see the world as violent, rather than appreciating that it is *less* violent than it used to be. For Pinker, a number of important cultural changes that have occurred over the course of human history have shaped—and are still shaping—human psychology. These changes are making us less violent both as individuals and as a species.

Pinker uses statistical evidence to back his claim. His data includes figures for the deaths from wars, genocides,* and other large-scale violent events, as well as robberies and homicides across history.[4] He uses this to help identify the cultural and institutional forces that have caused the decline of violence. For Pinker these forces originate from the ideas of the "humanitarian Enlightenment,"* an intellectual movement that began in the eighteenth century, which placed a high value on human life. The Enlightenment helped to change society, and the social shifts it triggered also altered human psychology. The result, Pinker argues, was a decline in violence.

The Better Angels has several purposes. Pinker wants to counter the idea that violence is on the rise, noting that this common belief can have negative consequences: it prompts us to accept decisions based on fleeting impressions of danger, instead of decisions based on thought and reflection.[5] To correct this, Pinker provides an objective analysis of hard evidence and facts about the decline of violence. He also identifies the forces that have had an impact on this decrease, among which are the spread of democracy and the increasing tendency to see all human beings as citizens of a single community. In addition he points to changes in moral values and aesthetic tastes (that is, what might be considered "beautiful" or "ugly") that push us away from violence and toward pacifism.*

The Better Angels is descriptive. Pinker counters the idea that violence is rising by telling the story of how it has declined. He does so by identifying the trends of violence over history, and examines the reasons for the decrease by looking at historical changes. But *The Better Angels* also has a prescriptive* purpose: that is, Pinker discusses rules and tools that might be adopted to reduce violence further in the future.

Why Does *The Better Angels of Our Nature* Matter?

Published in 2011, *The Better Angels* soon became a controversial work. It was immediately reviewed in all the major journals and newspapers, including the *New York Times*, the *New Yorker*, the *Guardian*, the *Economist*, the *Wall Street Journal*, *Nature*, and the *Financial Times*. Pinker is still reiterating the main claims of the book via the media; it remains a topic of discussion in the academic world, as well as in politics, economics, and society at large.

Pinker's work has helped to reshape debates about violence in the social sciences* (studies that encompass fields as diverse as anthropology, psychology, law, and economics). It has provided a starting point for fresh ways of thinking about the history of violence and the reasons for its decline. And it has revived interest in the study of statistical trends related to violence and the factors that trigger (or limit) it. As a result, the tools and conceptual analysis employed by Pinker in *The Better Angels* can be used in other areas of research to deepen our knowledge of violence.

More broadly, the work has been read and discussed by figures outside academia who are interested in social change. The American entrepreneur and philanthropist Bill Gates* wrote in his blog that *The Better Angels* "stands out as one of the most important books I've read—not just this year, but ever."[6] In 2015, Mark Zuckerberg,* the founder of the social networking service Facebook, started a book club on Facebook. *The Better Angels* was the second title chosen for the 2015 "Year of Books." Such endorsements illustrate the importance of *The Better Angels*, its relevance to public debates, and the impact it could have on the world.

The influence of the book is twofold: first, it helps raise awareness of the most pressing issues to do with violence; second, Pinker's analysis can be used to search for solutions to the problem of violence: it could help us create policies that foster and reinforce the social trends that may reduce violence further in the future.

---

1. Steven Pinker, *The Blank Slate: The Modern Denial of Human Nature* (London: Penguin Books, 2002), 331.

2. Steven Pinker, *The Better Angels of Our Nature: Why Violence Has Declined* (London: Penguin Books, 2011), 331.

3. Steven Pinker, "Now For The Good News: Things Really Are Getting Better," *Guardian*, September 11, 2015, accessed December 19, 2015, http://www.theguardian.com/commentisfree/2015/sep/11/news-isis-syria-headlines-violence-steven-pinker.

4. Pinker, *The Better Angels*, 1–30.

5. Pinker, *The Better Angels*, xxi.

6. Bill Gates, "My Bookshelf: *The Better Angels of Our Nature: Why Violence Has Declined*," June 18, 2012, accessed December 29, 2015, http://www. gatesnotes.com/Books/The-Better-Angels-of-Our-Nature.

SECTION 1
INFLUENCES

THE AUTHOR AND THE HISTORICAL CONTEXT

KEY POINTS

* *The Better Angels* contains a comprehensive review of statistical data about the trends of violence.

* It argues that violence has declined in recent centuries and presents a bold thesis about the causes of this decline.

* The second half of the twentieth century was characterized by a long period of peace. Steven Pinker grew up during this time and this may have shaped his ideas about the decline of violence.

Why Read This Text?

Steven Pinker's *The Better Angels of Our Nature: Why Violence Has Declined* was published in 2011 and immediately sparked debate. The book discusses three key topics:

* The history of violence.
* The psychological* origins of violence.
* The institutional and cultural changes that can influence violence.

Pinker's thesis is that violence has declined over the course of history and that this decline will probably continue: "For all the violence that remains in the world, we are living in an extraordinary age ... [R] egardless of how the trends extrapolate into the future, something remarkable has brought us to the present."[1] He argues forcefully in favor of this positive outlook, using a large pool of data to support his arguments. And it is this combination of thought-provoking ideas, backed by his rigorous scientific methodology,* that makes the work important.

The impact of *The Better Angels* on the debate about violence is undeniable. All the major newspapers, including the *New Yorker*, the *New York Times*, the *Guardian*, and the *Financial Times*, have reviewed the book.[2] It has also started numerous academic and public discussions. Given its recent publication it is premature to predict its long-term influence on academic research, but its importance to current debate can be measured by the number of media references that have been made to it. As soon as a violent event hits the headlines, journalists contact Pinker for a reaction.[3] This happened after the rise of the Syrian conflict* in 2011, the start of the Ukrainian conflict* in 2013, and the 2015 attack on the satirical newspaper *Charlie Hebdo*.* In September 2015, Pinker published an opinion piece in the British newspaper the *Guardian* to claim that, despite these conflicts, violence is still in decline.[4]

> "This book grew out of an answer to the question, 'What are you optimistic about?' and I hope that the numbers I have marshaled have lifted your assessment of the state of the world from the lugubrious conventional wisdom."
>
> —— Steven Pinker, *The Better Angels of Our Nature: Why Violence Has Declined*

Author's Life

Steven Pinker was born in 1954 in Canada, the eldest of three children. His father was a lawyer and his mother a high-school vice-principal, while his brother now works as a policy analyst* in Canada (that is, he is engaged in determining the social consequences of public policy); both Steven Pinker and his sister are psychologists. The family is Jewish, but Pinker calls himself an atheist*5 and criticizes the role that religion can play in supporting violence.

After studying psychology at Dawson College and at McGill University in Montréal, Pinker completed a doctorate in experimental psychology* (the study of the human mind and behavior in ways that can be measured) at Harvard University, under the supervision of the American psychologist Stephen Kosslyn.* He still lives in the United States, and is now Harvard's Johnstone Family Professor. Married three times, his current wife is the American novelist Rebecca Goldstein.* He acknowledges her influence on *The Better Angels*—in particular her role in bringing to his attention the importance of the Enlightenment.*6 This was an intellectual movement with its roots in eighteenth-century Europe, characterized by the appeal to rationality and the defense of liberty, tolerance, and rights.

Prior to *The Better Angels*, Pinker was known for his work in the fields of psychology (the study of the human mind and behavior) and linguistics* (the study of the nature, history, and functioning of language); he published a number of academic texts and popular books. These helped to widen interest in the findings of cognitive science* (scientific inquiry into the operations, history, and faculties of the mind and brain), such as ideas about the origins of language and the functioning of our cognitive capacities. Pinker's scientific training provides the backbone for the statistical approach he uses in *The Better Angels*. This scientific methodology helps to support and strengthen the arguments in the book.

Author's Background

Every day, we hear news of conflict, war, homicides, and robberies. The first half of the twentieth century witnessed two world wars* and several genocides.* So it has become common to think of the twentieth century as the most devastating period in human history: an era of truly global conflict in which war reached new heights of destructiveness. The early twenty-first century, meanwhile, has seen the rise of modern dangers such as climate change* and terrorism.* With the world around us torn apart by regional conflicts, religious extremism, and natural disasters, many analysts warn about the dangers of our times: warnings that are amplified by the media. The British journalist Roger Cohen* writes, "We are vulnerable and we are fearful."[7]

Pinker was born in the mid-twentieth century, the history of which had an influence on his ideas about violence. Instead of endorsing the mainstream opinion that humanity is becoming ever more destructive, however, he refutes this view; his statistical analysis shows that it is possible to reach a different conclusion. Pinker's training in scientific psychology and his secular education have helped shape his willingness to challenge opinions. His starting point was to try to look at human history objectively. Doing this spurred him to ask "why [there] has been so much violence in the past" and "why it has come down."These, he states, are "the two psychological questions that got me going."[8]

1. Steven Pinker, *The Better Angels of Our Nature: Why Violence Has Declined* (London: Penguin Books, 2011), 480.

2. Steven Pinker, "Review Excerpts for *The Better Angels of Our Nature*," accessed December 29, 2015, http://stevenpinker.com/content/review-excerpts-better-angels-our-nature.

3. Steven Pinker, "Has the Decline of Violence Reversed since The Better Angels of Our Nature was Written?" accessed December 29, 2015, http://stevenpinker.com/files/pinker/files/has_the_decline_of_violence_reversed_since_the_better_angels_of_our_nature_was_written. pdf?m=1410709356.

4. Steven Pinker, "Now For The Good News: Things Really Are Getting Better," *Guardian*, September 11, 2015, accessed December 19, 2015, http://www.theguardian.com/commentisfree/2015/sep/11/news-isis-syria-headlines-violence-steven-pinker.

5. Steve Paulson, "Proud atheists," *Salon*, October 15, 2007, accessed December 29, 2015, http://www.salon.com/2007/10/15/pinker_goldstein/.

6. Steven Pinker, "Frequently Asked Questions about *The Better Angels of Our Nature: Why Violence Has Declined*," accessed December 29, 2015, http://stevenpinker.com/pages/frequently-asked-questions-about-better-angels-our-nature-why-violence-has-declined.

7. Roger Cohen, "A Climate of Fear," *New York Times*, October 27, 2014, accessed December 29, 2015, http://www.nytimes.com/2014/10/28/opinion/roger-cohen-a-climate-of-fear.html.

8. HSRP, "The Decline in Global Violence: Reality or Myth?" March 3, 2014, accessed December 29, 2015, http://www.hsrgroup.org/docs/Publications/HSR2013/HSR_2013_Press_Release.pdf.

MODULE 2
ACADEMIC CONTEXT

KEY POINTS

* The study of violence is a complex multidisciplinary field. It interests researchers in anthropology* (the study of human beings via research into culture, society, and belief), history, sociology* (the study of the functioning of society and social behavior), economics,* political science* (the study of political institutions and political behavior), psychology* (the study of the human mind and behavior), and moral philosophy* (inquiry into the nature of "right behavior" and ethics).

* Researchers focus on different aspects of violence, and their interest depends on their field of study. Some explore its historical development, others its causes, and others its biological roots.

* *The Better Angels* brings together research from history, anthropology, and psychology.

The Work in Its Context

Steven Pinker's book *The Better Angels of Our Nature: Why Violence Has Declined* draws on work from a range of disciplines. It brings together the work of researchers who have looked at the trends of violence over time, and the relationships between violence, psychology, and human nature.

Pinker became interested in looking at the statistics for violence after reading the work of the American political scientist Ted Robert Gurr.*[1] In 1981, Gurr published a graph showing how homicide rates in England had declined by 95 percent between the thirteenth and twentieth centuries. Other academics had also gathered statistical evidence about violence. Joshua Goldstein,[2] the eminent American scholar of international relations, had conducted research into the number of victims of wars, while the American political scientist Rudolph Rummel* had looked at the number of victims of genocides.*[3] Pinker used their data and methods in *The Better Angels*.

The study of violence raises several questions:

- How do we collect data about violence?
- How do we define violence?
- Can we infer any future trends about violence from the study of the past?
- Is violence an inherent aspect of human nature or is it the result of nurture (the environment, notably upbringing and parenting)?[4]

In other words,are humans born with certain characters and tendencies, or do they learn these as a result of their upbringing, society, and culture? Pinker starts his inquiry by examining this question, and later includes other issues.

His statistical approach also touches on issues concerning data: How is data collected? What do sets of data compare? What is the best way to collect data? Should data about other forms of aggression and conflict—domestic violence* or prison rates, for example—be studied? Political scientists and sociologists, as well as other academics, are currently debating which sources researchers should use.[5]

> *"[I]t was an interest in human nature and its moral and political implications, carried over from my earlier books ... Then in 2007, through a quirky chain of events, I was contacted by scholars in a number of fields who informed me there was far more evidence for a decline in violence than I had realized. Their data convinced me that the decline of violence deserved a book of its own."*
>
> —— Steven Pinker, "Frequently Asked Questions about *The Better Angels of Our Nature: Why Violence Has Declined*"

Overview of the Field

The discussion about the interaction between nature and nurture* has a long history. The seventeenth-century English philosopher Thomas Hobbes* (1588–1679) thought that humans have an innate tendency to fight one another. Hobbes argued that only the presence of a strong state (the "Leviathan") can prevent permanent war.[6] In contrast, the eighteenth-century Geneva-born philosopher Jean-Jacques Rousseau* (1712–78) is credited with the development of the myth of the "noble savage."* This was the idea that when living in a state of nature* (in a band, or tribe, rather than in a state), humans are intrinsically good.[7]

These thinkers still influence contemporary anthropology, sociology, and psychology. Early anthropologists such as the Scottish diplomat John Crawfurd* were influenced by the notion of the "noble savage"; this continues to permeate some areas of current enquiry.[8] Other thinkers, such as the American scientist and historian Jared Diamond,* follow Hobbes and emphasize the brutality of the state of nature. These academics tend to characterize societies organized along non-state lines as living in a condition of perpetual conflict. The same divisions are seen in psychology. For those who subscribe to the empiricist* perspective, according to which knowledge comes from experience alone, humans are born as "blank slates"—all our psychological faculties, including violence, are acquired by means of "nurture." Countering this, the nativist* perspective argues that humans are born with some faculties,abilities,and bodies of knowledge.

In *The Better Angels* Pinker positions himself on the side of Hobbes, Diamond, and the nativists. But unlike Hobbes, Pinker does not think that human nature is intrinsically evil or inflexible; for him, it contains the psychological seeds both of violence and peaceable behavior. Nor does he consider the state to be the only entity that can reduce violence. For Pinker, this reduction can be traced to a change of attitude about the value of human life, which started with the cultural emphasis on reason and liberty produced by the intellectual and cultural current known as the Enlightenment* in the eighteenth century.

Academic Influences

Pinker's inspiration came from a group of thinkers loosely connected by a shared core of ideas, rather than from a full-blown school of thought. He acknowledges, in particular, two very different figures as his primary influences: the English mathematician Lewis Fry Richardson* and the German-born sociologist* Norbert Elias.*

Lewis Richardson was an applied mathematician (roughly,

a mathematician who conducts research for practical purposes), mostly known for his work on weather prediction. He was also one of the people who initiated the use of mathematical analysis in studying armed violence.[9] Pinker adopts Richardson's method of statistical analysis in exploring the history of violence.

From Norbert Elias, Pinker obtains his outlook on history. In his book *The Civilizing Process*, Elias puts forward the idea that since the end of the Middle Ages* there has been an increasing process of civilization in Europe, evidenced by changes of attitude toward violent behaviors, strengthening of social connectedness, and an increase in self-control. Elias identifies the forces that brought about this process of civilization and argues that it has resulted in a change in human psychology.[10]

Following in Elias's steps, Pinker tries to find the external causes that have transformed psychology and made humans less violent. He argues that ideas become integrated in social institutions and start to influence human psychology.[11] This blend of culture and cognitive psychology* (inquiry into mental processes such as thought, creativity, and memory) allows Pinker to bring nurture and nature back together.

---

1. Steven Pinker, *The Better Angels of Our Nature: Why Violence Has Declined* (London: Penguin Books, 2011), 60.

2. Joshua Goldstein, *Winning the War on War: The Surprising Decline in Armed Conflict Worldwide* (New York: Dutton, 2011).

3. Rudolph Rummel, *Death by Government* (New Brunswick, NJ: Transaction, 1994).

4. Nils Petter Gleditsch et al., "The Forum: The Decline of War," *International Studies Review* 15, no. 3 (2013): 396–419.

5. Gleditsch et al., "The Forum," 396–419.

6. Thomas Hobbes, *Leviathan* (Oxford: Clarendon Press, 2012).

7. Jean-Jacques Rousseau, *Discourse on the Origin of Inequality*, trans. Franklin Philip (Oxford: Oxford's World Classics, 2009).

8. Ted Ellingson, *The Myth of the Noble Savage* (Berkeley: University of California Press, 2001).

9. Lewis Fry Richardson, *Statistics of Deadly Quarrels* (Pittsburgh: Boxwood Press, 1960).

10. Norbert Elias, *The Civilizing Process*, trans. Edmund Jephcott (New York: Pantheon Books, 1982).

11. Pinker, *The Better Angels*, 694–6.

MODULE 3
THE PROBLEM

KEY POINTS

* A central question for thinkers studying violence is: Can violence decrease over time, or is human nature too deeply connected to violent instincts to change?

* Steven Pinker takes the optimistic world view that violence has been declining, supporting his arguments with a statistical analysis of crimes, wars, and other violent events over the course of history.

* Pinker also proposes a theory about why and how violence has declined.

Core Question

At the heart of Steven Pinker's book *The Better Angels of Our Nature: Why Violence Has Declined* is the question as to *why* it has declined. While the longest section of his work is devoted to the data that demonstrates the decrease, Pinker is not interested solely in trends, but in what causes them. He argues that while humans do have a psychological tendency to engage in conflict, they also possess the psychological ability to prevent violence. He goes on to explore the environmental and societal forces that have caused the decline, despite the existence of a certain inclination toward aggression.

Pinker was not the first thinker to look at the historical trends of violence. He says that his interest in this area was inspired by a book written by the Canadian evolutionary psychologists* Martin

Daly* and Margo Wilson* (evolutionary psychology is the study of human and nonhuman psychology from the perspective of modern evolutionary theory). In *Homicide* (1988) Daly and Wilson suggest that violent deaths have declined over the course of history. More recently this claim has been discussed and accepted more widely.[1]

Yet this idea can seem counterintuitive when looked at in the context of twentieth-century history—a period that witnessed two world wars,* genocides,* colonialism* (the exploitation and political domination of a land and people by a foreign power or people), and terrorism.* These events resulted in the commonly shared view that we are living in the most violent epoch of world history. Pinker's work directly challenges this belief. His originality lies in his argument that the decline of violence can be traced to changes in our values and our institutions. These, in turn, have influenced human psychology.

> "But it is just as foolish to let our lurid imaginations determine our sense of the probabilities ... The numbers tell us that war, genocide, and terrorism have declined over the past two decades—not to zero, but by a lot ... The conditions that favored this happy outcome—democracy, prosperity, decent government, peacekeeping, open economies, and the decline of antihuman ideologies—are not, of course, guaranteed to last forever. But nor are they likely to vanish overnight."
>
> —— Steven Pinker, *The Better Angels of Our Nature: Why Violence Has Declined*

The Participants

The problem of violence is at the heart of many political and societal debates, as well as being of interest to academics across many different fields. Historians tend to study the numerical data on violence; for example, the French historian Robert Muchembled* explores the trends of violence from the later Middle Ages* to the present day, and tries to find the roots of its decline. Like Pinker, he is interested in the ways in which male aggression has been tamed, and points to this as a reason.[2]

Anthropologists* have studied many aspects of violence, including its origins in human lineage and its development in various communities,[3] while evolutionary psychologists have attempted to find the biological and psychological roots of violence. Evolutionary psychologists also study the mechanisms (like morality) that aim to diminish conflict.[4] The American husband and wife team John Tooby* and Leda Cosmides* are pioneers in the field of evolutionary psychology. They have explored at length how our "natural instincts" and the modes of thought we learn from modern society interact and collide.

These are only a few examples of the participants in a vast field of study and public debate. But despite the many voices involved, the debate itself centers on very few oft-repeated claims and arguments.

The Contemporary Debate

There are two broad debates in contemporary research. The first is about numbers: Is violence increasing or decreasing? The second is about the origins of violence: Where does violence come from—human biology, or society?

There is a view that attributes violence to society alone. Pinker aims to refute this. In 2000, 11 years before the publication of *The Better Angels*, he wrote a piece for the *New York Times* in which he stated, "The prevailing wisdom among many intellectuals has been that evil has nothing to do with human nature and must be attributed to political institutions."[5]

He goes on to challenge this, arguing that violence is part of human nature. But at the same time he tries to avoid the negative conclusions of this view by attempting to find a middle ground. He argues that if violence is part of human nature, it can be tamed by history and society. Pinker suggests that the rational ideas of the Enlightenment* were key to this possibility. This view is similar to that of the British theoretical physicist David Deutsch.* In Pinker's words, Deutsch "defends the unfashionable view that the Enlightenment inaugurated an era of unlimited intellectual and moral progress."[6]

1. For example, John Mueller, "War Has Almost Ceased to Exist: An Assessment," *Political Science Quarterly* 124, no. 2 (2009): 297–321.

2. Robert Muchembled, *A History of Violence: From the End of the Middle Ages to the Present* (Cambridge: Polity Press, 2012).

3. Bettina Schmidt and Ingo Schröder, *Anthropology of Violence and Conflict* (New York: Psychology Press, 2001).

4. John Tooby and Leda Cosmides, "Groups in Mind: The Coalitional Roots of War and Morality," in *Human Morality and Sociality: Evolutionary and Comparative Perspectives*, ed. Henrik Hogh-Olesen (New York: Palgrave Macmillan, 2010), 91–234.

5. Steven Pinker, "All about Evil," *New York Times*, October 29, 2000, accessed December 22, 2015, http://www.nytimes.com/2000/10/29/books/all-about-evil.html.

6. Steven Pinker, "Stephen Pinker: By the Book," *New York Times: The Sunday Book Review*, September 25, 2014, accessed December 22, 2015, http://www.nytimes.com/2014/09/28/books/review/steven-pinker-by-the-book. html.

THE AUTHOR'S CONTRIBUTION

KEY POINTS

* Pinker has a balanced view of the origins of violence. He argues that some aspects of human psychology* tend toward violence, but that cultural and institutional forces can inhibit these tendencies.

* Pinker uses data from many sources to investigate levels of violence, both current and in the past.

* Pinker's moderate answer provides a proportionate view of the nature—nurture* debate: while violence is part of our human nature, external forces (nurture) can affect this.

Author's Aims

In *The Better Angels of Our Nature: How Violence Has Declined*, Steven Pinker aims to challenge two assumptions about violence and human nature. The first is that violence has been steadily growing over the course of history.[1] The second is that we should be negative about the human condition. Pinker argues that while we are born with certain tendencies—an innate biological core of human psychology—this does not mean we are doomed to revert to violence. He challenges this "equation between a belief in a human nature and fatalism about the human condition."[2]

Pinker begins to build a complex but coherent picture of the interaction between psychology and the history of violence by presenting an overview of the data. He goes on to discuss the psychological factors that can encourage or inhibit violence. Finally he brings these discussions together and argues that over the centuries, human violence has declined, and that this decline is due to external forces that have tamed the human inclination toward violence—without eradicating it. This method allows him to redefine the question concerning the origins and decline of violence in terms of a complex interaction between internal (psychological) and external (institutional and cultural) factors.

Pinker partially achieves his aims in *The Better Angels*. The statistical trends he presents, though disputed, do show some decline in violence. And his claims about the interaction between history and psychology—while controversial—do have some coherence.

> *"It's a natural topic for anyone interested in human nature. The question,'Is our species innately violent and war-loving, or innately peaceful and cooperative?' goes back literally hundreds of years, maybe thousands. So it naturally falls under the category of psychology ... The worry is: if violence is in the genes—if we're killer apes and we have homicidal DNA—then there's nothing you can do about it. But this is a non sequitur. The answer is no, we don't have to be fatalistic."*
>
> —— Steven Pinker, interview in *Skeptical Inquirer*

Approach

Pinker takes an analytical approach in *The Better Angels*, starting from definitions, examining large collections of data, and then interpreting these in the light of his proposal. His definition of "violence" is any physical force used to cause damage or injury to others, excluding metaphorical violence, such as verbal aggression. He examines data in relation to two kinds of physical violence: that committed by private citizens (homicide, robbery, assault, and so on) and that committed by institutions (war, genocide,* capital punishment, and the like).

His data is gathered from various sources: forensic archeology (that is, archeology based on the analytical methods used at a crime scene) and ethnography* (the study of culture); town records; and the Uppsala Conflict Data Project and the Peace Research Institute in Oslo (resources hosted in Sweden and Norway respectively, which provide useful statistical and analytical information about violence and conflict resolution). In some cases, he uses data from historians and political scientists working on wars and genocides. Pinker always tries to be rigorous in his choice of data, stating his aim "was to use data only from sources that had a commitment to objectivity."[3] It is also important to note that he calculates the *relative* rate of violent crimes and not the absolute numbers. In other words, he calculates the number of victims of violence as a proportion of the population size. While there are more violent deaths now than in the past, this number has to be measured against the total size of the population. When the latter is taken into account, Pinker shows that there are far fewer violent deaths now than there were in the past.

Finally, Pinker uses ideas from philosophy,* sociology,* and psychology to uncover the bigger trends revealed by the data. Chief among these is the work of the German-born sociologist Norbert

Elias.* Pinker uses Elias's book *The Civilizing Process* to explore the societal changes that have triggered the reduction of violence.

Contribution in Context

The Better Angels is a highly original work in respect of its breadth, complexity, and interdisciplinary nature (the way it draws on the aims and methods of different academic disciplines). Pinker borrows the methodology of military historians and sociologists to gather data about violence. He then considers his findings using the methodology of evolutionary psychology* to examine how trends in the history of violence connect with human psychology.

The originality of the work stems from Pinker's ability to put together conceptual claims with empirical* data (that is, data verifiable by observation):

- While historians were gathering data that pointed to the decline of violence, they did not suggest any psychological interpretation of this trend.
- Psychologists were studying the biological roots of violence and the ways in which these factors could be changed.
- Some moral philosophers* were arguing that moral progress is being made, but without basing their claims on data.

In *The Better Angels* Pinker manages to bring all these lines of research together in a coherent argument.

While Pinker has been part of the field of cognitive science* (interdisciplinary inquiry into the mind and brain, often drawing on fields such as philosophy, neuroscience, and linguistics), he positions himself more as an independent thinker who does not belong in a strict sense to any school of thought. He nonetheless acknowledges his debt to many theorists, and says he is inspired by "humanitarian Enlightenment": * a secular and rational approach to inquiry, based on science.

---

1. Steven Pinker, *The Better Angels of Our Nature: Why Violence Has Declined* (London: Penguin Books, 2011), xxi–xxv.
2. Steven Pinker, "Frequently Asked Questions about *The Better Angels of Our Nature: Why Violence Has Declined*," accessed December 29, 2015, http://stevenpinker.com/pages/frequently-asked-questions-about-better-angels-our-nature-why-violence-has-declined.
3. Pinker, "Frequently Asked Questions."

SECTION 2
IDEAS

MAIN IDEAS

KEY POINTS

* Pinker sums up the psychological* roots of both human violence and peaceable nature by saying we possess "five demons and four Better Angels."
* He identifies our four "Better Angels" as empathy,* self-control, moral sense, and the faculty of reason.
* Pinker uses data and statistics because he wants to provide an objective analysis of the phenomenon of violence.

Key Themes

In *The Better Angels of Our Nature: How Violence Has Declined*, Steven Pinker argues that violence has declined over the course of human history—a proposal contrasting with the popular impression that violence is increasing. As Pinker writes, "I have to convince you that violence really has gone down over the course of history, knowing that the very idea invites skepticism, incredulity, and sometimes anger."[1] To do so, he states, only hard evidence will help: "I will have to persuade you with numbers."[2]

The decrease in violence applies to both large-scale violence (conflict between states and nations), and small-scale violence (conflict within families and communities). Pinker offers a broad historical overview of the trend, spanning millennia. He begins his ambitious historical inquiry with prehistoric hunter-gatherers* (people who lived by hunting and collecting rather than developing agriculture) before turning to the Middle Ages* and arguing persuasively that medieval* society was permeated by violence. He continues to contemporary history and claims that despite two world wars,* the twentieth century saw a decline in violence.

Pinker then explores human psychology in an attempt to uncover the forces that have made us more peaceable. He identifies two opposing psychological forces: we are pushed toward violence by our "inner demons," and urged to cooperate and live in peace by the "The Better Angels of our nature" (an expression borrowed from the nineteenth-century American president Abraham Lincoln).* According to Pinker, psychology reveals that humans are neither intrinsically good nor intrinsically evil. On the contrary, "Human nature accommodates motives that impel us to violence ... but also motives that ... impel us toward peace."[3]

In the final part of the book, Pinker puts history and psychology together. He examines the external forces that have transformed (and are transforming) human psychology.

> "[V]iolence has declined over long stretches of time, and today we may be living in the most peaceable era in our species' existence ... The historical trajectory of violence affects not only how life is lived but how it is understood. What could be more fundamental to our sense of meaning and purpose than a conception of whether the strivings of the human race over long stretches of time have left us better or worse off?"
>
> ——Steven Pinker, *The Better Angels of Our Nature: How Violence Has Declined*

Exploring the Ideas

Pinker outlines six historical transitions that have contributed to the decline of violence. The most important ones are:

- The "civilizing process"*—a term borrowed from the German-born sociologist* Norbert Elias* to denote a set of changes in institutions, values, and sensibilities that started in the Middle Ages, and helped to create more peaceful social attitudes.
- The "humanitarian revolution"—the appearance of a culture of pacifism,* tolerance, and secularism in eighteenth-century Europe, ushered in by the Enlightenment.*

Alongside these two fundamental historical forces Pinker identifies four other trends that have helped reduce violence:

- The absence of wars in Europe and the United States since World War II.*
- The decline in conflicts all over the world over the past 30 years.
- Stable economies.

Pinker then looks at psychology. Here he identifies two opposing forces: the "five inner demons" that drive us toward violence and the "four Better Angels" that guide us toward peace and cooperation. He points out that from a psychological point of view,"aggression" is not a unified phenomenon but originates in five different psychological forces (the so-called demons). The "four Better Angels" are the psychological qualities that enable us to foster cooperation and altruism, or selfless behavior: empathy, self-control, moral sense, and the faculty of reason.

Looking at the interaction between history and psychology, Pinker identifies five external forces that have shaped human psychology and are driving the decline of violence:

- The presence of a strong state (in the governmental sense) that has an effective monopoly on violent action (through, for example, the police or military).
- The development of international commerce that requires peaceful exchange and stability.
- The increasing respect given to women and what are sometimes understood to be female values.
- The rise of modern means of transportation and communication.
- The increasing attention paid to rational, reasoned argument.

Together these forces encourage humans to listen to their "Better Angels" and silence their "inner demons."

Language and Expression

The Better Angels is extremely well researched. Pinker's conclusions are based on extensive inquiry, facts, graphs, figures, and data. Despite this, the book is easy to read and the tone is accessible, conversational, or in Pinker's terms, "at times irreverent."[4] The book is intended for the general public, not only for specialists. Pinker's ambition is to reach a wide audience as well as to have an impact on current scholarship on violence and to foster academic debate and research.

Nevertheless, the work does use statistical tools, so a reader without any training in statistics might not fully understand how the data has been gathered and analyzed. But it is always explained and discussed, and the statistics used are fairly intuitive. In Pinker's words,"I will have to persuade you with numbers, which I will glean from datasets and depict in graphs. In each case I'll explain where the numbers came from and do my best to interpret the ways they fall into place."[5]

The colloquial language and the use of anecdotes, sometimes taken from Pinker's life (he characterizes the book, for example, as a "tale of six trends, five inner demons, four better angels, and five historical forces"[6]) make the overall argument easy to understand and follow.

1. Steven Pinker, *The Better Angels of Our Nature: Why Violence Has Declined* (London: Penguin Books, 2011), xxii.
2. Pinker, *The Better Angels*, xxii.
3. Pinker, *The Better Angels*, 483.
4. Pinker, *The Better Angels*, 696.
5. Pinker, *The Better Angels*, xxii.
6. Pinker, *The Better Angels*, xxiv.

MODULE 6
SECONDARY IDEAS

KEY POINTS

• *The Better Angels* examines the relationship between religion, ideology,* and violence. (An ideology is a system of norms, beliefs, and theories held by a group or by individuals.)

• Pinker also evaluates the role of biology in prompting or reducing violence. He makes specific references to gender* differences—a theme largely overlooked in the debates that followed his work.

• Pinker's evaluation of the evolution of violence has had an impact on discussions in the field of evolutionary psychology.*

Other Ideas

Steven Pinker's *The Better Angels of Our Nature: Why Violence Has Declined* is a complex work with a number of interconnected ideas; in it, Pinker also discusses many secondary ideas.

One of his key secondary ideas concerns the role of religion in the history of violence. While some thinkers claim that the Christian* religion has played a major role in fighting violence, Pinker opposes this view, instead looking at the Crusades* (the invasions of the Middle East by European Christian armies in the medieval* period) and the Inquisition* (an institution established by the Christian Church in the thirteenth century to ensure the purity of belief and religious practice, later notorious for the use of torture in the extraction of confessions) to underline its role in initiating conflicts and persecutions. His main claim in the book is that a secular* (nonreligious) process led to the development of secular liberal democracies* and to a reduction in violence.

Another important secondary issue is whether we have *evolved* as a species to be less violent. Pinker asks whether there has been a selection of traits that has favored peaceable individuals over violent ones, or whether human nature has remained unchanged over time. Although Pinker considers several pieces of evidence that could potentially support the idea that biological evolution* alters core human impulses, he ultimately rejects this idea. He explains that "while recent biological evolution may, in theory, have tweaked our inclinations toward violence and nonviolence, we have no good evidence that it actually has ... At least for the time being [therefore], we have no need for that hypothesis."[1] His ultimate position is that human biology has remained unchanged over the timespan of the decline of violence (around 10,000 years).

> *"When it comes to the history of violence, the significant distinction is not one between theistic and atheistic regimes. It's the one between regimes that were based on demonizing, utopian ideologies (including Nazism, and militant religions) and secular liberal democracies that are based on the ideal of human rights."*
>
> ——Steve Pinker, "Frequently Asked Questions about *The Better Angels of Our Nature: Why Violence Has Declined*"

Exploring the Ideas

Pinker responds to this by saying that it is not the fact that these regimes were atheistic that caused their violence, but the fact that they were all supported by a totalitarian ideology—their governments interceded in the lives of their citizens, aggressively suppressing dissent, as a point of political philosophy. In other words, they were driven by a doctrine that endorsed their violent behavior (for the Nazis, this was a belief in certain forms of racial superiority). Pinker argues that the doctrine-driven nature of the major totalitarian regimes gives them a fundamental similarity to religion. He goes on to contrast ideology-based regimes (both religious and nonreligious) with secular liberal democracies (the system of government dominant in the West today). He contends that it is within secular liberal democracies that violence declines.

While Pinker rejects the idea that nonviolent traits have evolved, he does consider how malleable human biology may be (that is, how easily it can be molded). The answer to this has consequences for the malleability of human psychology.* Pinker's position is that there is some degree of pliability, but that this mostly stems from how far the environment is able to favor the "Better Angels" over our "inner demons."

Overlooked

One secondary idea that has been overlooked following the publication of *The Better Angels* is Pinker's discussion of the relationship between gender differences and violence. Males statistically show a greater propensity to violence than females. Pinker writes that "The rise and fall of testosterone* over the life span correlates, more or less, with the rise and fall of male pugnacity."*2 (Pugnacity is the tendency to be aggressive.)

Pinker's view is that there are psychological (and biological) factors that make men more prone to violence. This does not mean that all men are violent, but it is to say that some biological factors make men more prone to aggression in some cultural and social contexts. Going on from this, Pinker argues that the "feminization" of society has been a factor in reducing violence. By feminization he means both the increase in the value accorded to "feminine qualities" (such as empathy)* and the political empowerment of women. This political empowerment includes developments such as an end to marriages in which the male partner holds all the power, the right of girls to be born, and women's control over reproduction.

The issue of gender difference is still a hot topic today. Pinker endorses "equity feminism": * the idea of legal equality between the sexes, according to which men and women should, for example, receive the same salary for doing the same work. But he argues that there are both biological and psychological differences between the genders;3 in his book *The Blank Slate* (2002), he writes that "women and men do not have interchangeable minds ... people have desires other than power ..."4

In *The Better Angels*, Pinker discusses gender differences and their role in the history of violence. As well as offering insights into possible measures for reducing violence, his ideas could have an important impact in areas such as education.

1. Steven Pinker, *The Better Angels of Our Nature: Why Violence Has Declined* (London: Penguin Books, 2011), 620−1.
2. Pinker, *The Better Angels*, 519.
3. Steven Pinker and Elizabeth Spelke, "The Science of Gender and Science. Pinker vs. Spelke," *Edge: The Third Culture*, May 16, 2005, accessed December 22, 2015, Edge.org/3rd_culture/debate05/debate05_index.html.
4. Steven Pinker, *The Blank Slate: The Modern Denial of Human Nature* (London: Penguin Books, 2002), 343.

ACHIEVEMENT

KEY POINTS

- *The Better Angels* challenges a pessimistic view of history by providing robust statistical data about the decline of violence over the course of human history.

- It also aims to discover the cultural and psychological* causes behind the decline in violence. Pinker's achievements in this regard are disputed.

- One issue with Pinker's data is that it is mostly limited to the Western world.

Assessing the Argument

In writing *The Better Angels of Our Nature: Why Violence Has Declined*, Steven Pinker had two clear aims. He wanted to show that violence has been steadily declining over time, despite our impressions to the contrary. And he wanted to discover the reasons behind that decline.

Pinker's first aim is achieved through an impressive marshaling of data. The book contains around 100 graphs[1] gathered from a variety of sources. These show a downward trend in violence, both on a small scale (in families and communities) and a large scale (among nations and states). Pinker is also successful in explaining why—despite the data—we have the impression that violence is growing: "If you base your beliefs about the state of the world on what you read in the news, your beliefs will be incorrect. [It's] about things that happen, particularly bad things—and [given]]the nature of human cognition [people] base their estimates of risk on how easily they can recall examples from memory."[2]

Pinker's second aim was to discover *why* violence has declined. He attributes this to the emergence of cultural and institutional forces such as democracy,* the growth of economic exchanges and of cosmopolitanism*—the belief that all human beings are citizens of a single community—which leads to an increase in cultural and information exchange. These forces have led to institutional changes that support more peaceful societies.

In this regard, Pinker's thesis remains possible, but not proven. Violence is a complex and multifaceted phenomenon. As a result, we lack robust scientific evidence that shows the impact of institutional changes on the decline of violence. This is not to say that Pinker's thesis is false. His thesis shows that the decline in violence *correlates* (perhaps robustly) with some cultural changes. But he is not able to establish unequivocally that these changes were responsible for the decline of violence.

> *"The Better Angels of Our Nature is a supremely important book. To have command of so much research, spread across so many different fields, is a masterly achievement. Pinker convincingly demonstrates that there has been a dramatic decline in violence, and he is persuasive about the causes of that decline."*
>
> —— Peter Singer, *Is Violence History?*

Achievement in Context

The Better Angels has been an undeniable commercial success: a bestseller that sparked a vigorous debate. Its success was probably boosted by its timely publication in 2011. This coincided with the popular uprisings in the Middle East and North Africa that began in 2010 known as the Arab Spring* and the death of the terrorist leader Osama bin Laden: * two events that seemed—at the time— to support Pinker's claims.

Pinker's thesis that violence is in decline is based on empirical* data: observed, factual information. As with all truly empirical claims, it is open to falsification (being proven wrong). This means that the validity and achievement of this work depends on data continuing to support it.

In relation to this, Pinker recently examined new data that had been gathered between 2011 and 2015. He concluded that "[the] global trends since the completion of *The Better Angels of Our Nature* show no reversal of the historical decline of violence, and in every case except the effects of the conflict in Syria,* a continuation of the decline."[3]

Despite its limitations, *The Better Angels* is an achievement. Maybe the most balanced assessment of its success comes from the British political scientist Adam Roberts,* who wrote that "with all its imperfections, [the book] is much the most interesting work available on the terrifying subject of violence in history. It may be meta-history, but it is wonderfully illuminating."

Limitations

The Better Angels does have some shortcomings, however. These are evident both in the data Pinker has analyzed and in the conceptual framework he employs.

The data poses three key problems:

- Pinker compares data on violent deaths in timeframes that are distant from each other, such as the eighteenth and the twentieth century. This is problematic because we have only limited records of events in the past, and because comparing two very distant and different periods is necessarily based on an oversimplification of conditions and circumstances.
- Pinker does not always take into account deaths that are *indirectly* caused by wars. The Australian academic Jeff Lewis* challenges this exclusion of data on after-war mortality. He notes that wars always trigger follow-on civilian deaths, due to the lowering of living standards, sickness, and suicides. The inclusion of such data would increase the war mortality rate.
- Pinker's dataset is geographically limited, mostly to the United States and Europe; the rest of the world is largely overlooked. The American journalist Elizabeth Kolbert* writes,"The scope of Pinker's attentions is almost entirely confined to Western Europe."[4] She criticizes the absence of a discussion of the violence inherent in colonialism* (the exploitation of one territory and people by a dominant foreign power or people) and its impact on the colonized countries.

Another limitation of the book is Pinker's definition of violence, which is any use of physical force used to cause damage or injury in others. He does not include verbal, metaphorical, or economic violence. Even more importantly, he does not include the deeds of democratic states that could be regarded as state violence, such as increasing imprisonment rates in the United States and the mistreatment of prison inmates. This limited definition may have an impact on the scope of Pinker's claims.

---

1. Steven Pinker, "Graphic Evidence: Steven Pinker's Optimism on Trial," *Guardian*, September 11, 2015, accessed December 22, 2015, http://www.theguardian.com/commentisfree/ng-interactive/2015/sep/11/graphic-evidence-steven-pinkers-optimism-on-trial.

2. Steven Pinker, "Has the Decline of Violence Reversed since *The Better Angels of Our Nature* was Written?" accessed December 22, 2015, http://stevenpinker.com/files/pinker/files/has_the_decline_of_violence_reversed_since_the_better_angels_of_our_nature_was_written. pdf?m=1410709356.

3. Pinker, "Has the Decline of Violence Reversed?"

4. Elizabeth Kolbert, "Peace in Our Time: Steven Pinker's History of Violence," *New Yorker*, October 3, 2011, accessed December 22, 2015, http://www. newyorker.com/magazine/2011/10/03/peace-in-our-time-elizabeth-kolbert.

MODULE 8
PLACE IN THE AUTHOR'S WORK

KEY POINTS

* Pinker's body of work has focused on human psychology,* its functioning, and its evolutionary origins.
* *The Better Angels* is Pinker's 13th book and one of his most controversial best sellers.
* *The Better Angels* connects Pinker's work on the functioning of human psychology with a broader exploration of history and culture.

Positioning

When *The Better Angels of Our Nature: Why Violence Has Declined* was published in 2011, Steven Pinker was already known as one of the most influential authors of popular books on cognitive science.* *The Better Angels* is more ambitious than his previous works: Pinker steps outside of his area of expertise (cognitive science)* to integrate psychology with history, sociology,* and economics.* Pinker has explained in several interviews that he has been thinking about the issues discussed in *The Better Angels* since at least 2007. Its subject matter connects with his exploration of human nature in two of his earlier books, *The Blank Slate: The Modern Denial of Human Nature* (2002) and *The Stuff of Thought: Language as a Window into Human Nature* (2007).[1]

While Pinker has frequently discussed the issues of the book over the past four years, he has not written a major publication on the topic of violence since *The Better Angels*. His most recent work is *The Sense of Style: The Thinking Person's Guide to Writing in the 21st Century* (2014). As the title suggests, it aims to help people achieve a clear and accessible writing style. This is a departure from previous subjects he has explored, but like his earlier books, *The Sense of Style* is profoundly informed by up-to-date research in psychology and science.

> *"Human nature is a complex system with many components. It comprises mental faculties that lead us to violence, but also faculties that pull us away from violence, such as empathy, self-control, and a sense of fairness. It also comes equipped with open-ended combinatorial faculties for language and reasoning, which allow us to reflect on our condition and figure out better ways to live our lives. This vision of psychology, together with a commitment to secular humanism, has been a constant in my books, though it has become clearer to me in recent years."*
>
> ——Steve Pinker, "Frequently Asked Questions about *The Better Angels of Our Nature: Why Violence Has Declined*"

Integration

The main focus of Pinker's career has been human psychology and its place in nature and society. *The Better Angels* expands this, integrating the question of human psychology into a broader historical context. In this respect it is one of his most ambitious works.

Pinker's early works looked at experimental psychology* (the study of the human mind and behavior using scientific methodology) and linguistics* (the study of the various things that together serve to define language). He worked with the American cognitive scientist Stephen Kosslyn* on mental imagery (the way we represent the world to ourselves) and the representation of three-dimensional space. Later he looked at how infants acquire irregular verbs when learning language. His research on this was popularized in his *Words and Rules: The Ingredients of Language* (1999).[2]

By then, Pinker had already produced two best sellers. His first was *The Language Instinct* (1994), which introduced the American linguist Noam Chomsky's* work on language to a popular audience. Chomsky argues that the rules of language are innate: learning only triggers something that was already present and stored in the mind. Pinker defends this view against the opposing idea: that we are born as a clean slate and that language is a social construct imposed from outside.

In 1997 he produced another best seller, *How the Mind Works*. This, along with *The Blank Slate: The Modern Denial of Human Nature* (2002) and *The Stuff of Thought: Language as a Window into Human Nature* (2007) focuses on psychology more generally. These books introduce the ideas of contemporary experimental cognitive science and evolutionary psychology* to the public.

The Blank Slate anticipates some of the ideas discussed in *The Better Angels*. In this book Pinker refutes the idea that the mind is an empty canvas ready to be filled in by culture and society. He argues that it is shaped by evolution,* and fixed. Society has only a limited ability to change it: "The denial of human nature has spread beyond the academy and has led to a disconnect between intellectual life and common sense."[3] In *The Better Angels*, he again explores the relationship between evolution and psychology.

Significance

The Better Angels helped to establish Pinker as one of the most influential thinkers of our time. Given the variety of topics and fields he has worked in, it is not easy to establish whether this title is his best or most important work. It is difficult, for instance, to compare it to his academic research on mental imagery or on children's acquisition of irregular verbs. But what is certain is that while Pinker's scientific work and popular books about psychology made him an acclaimed cognitive scientist, *The Better Angels* established him as a global thinker. Indeed, in 2013 he was named the third most influential thinker of the year by *Prospect* magazine. As the British journalist John Dugdale writes,"Pinker might well have made the chart anyway, but probably owes his high position to his switch from his specialist field of psycholinguistics to history in *The Better Angels of Our Nature*."[4] In 2014 he was rated number 26 among the top 100 thinkers by the American bimonthly magazine *Foreign Policy*.[5]

As these references show, *The Better Angels* helped establish Pinker's fame beyond his original field of expertise. He is now at the center of debates on the most pressing contemporary issues.

1. Steven Pinker, "Frequently Asked questions About *The Better Angels of Our Nature: Why Violence Has Declined*," accessed December 22, 2015, http://stevenpinker.com/pages/frequently-asked-questions-about-better-angels-our-nature-why-violence-has-declined, accessed September 15, 2015.

2. Steven Pinker, *Words and Rules: The Ingredients of Language* (New York: HarperCollins, 1999).

3. Steven Pinker, *The Blank Slate: The Modern Denial of Human Nature* (London: Penguin, 2002), 14.

4. John Dugdale, "Richard Dawkins Named World's Top Thinker in Poll," *Guardian*, April 23, 2013, accessed December 22, 2015, http://www. theguardian.com/books/booksblog/2013/apr/25/richard-dawkins-named-top-thinker.

5. *Foreign Policy*, "A World Disrupted: The Leading Global Thinkers of 2014," accessed December 30, 2015, http://globalthinkers.foreignpolicy.com.

SECTION 3
IMPACT

THE FIRST RESPONSES

KEY POINTS

* The reaction to *The Better Angels* was polarized. The negative reviews disputed either Pinker's conceptual assumptions or his use and interpretation of the data.

* Pinker has replied to some of these criticisms in journal articles and interviews, either by presenting more data or by restating his conceptual points.

* Many of his critics remain unconvinced by his replies: their reactions allow for a more balanced view of the book.

Criticism

Steven Pinker's *The Better Angels of Our Nature: Why Violence has Declined* received mixed reviews.[1] The Australian moral philosopher* Peter Singer* called it a "supremely important book,"[2] while the American political scientist Robert Jervis* finds that the trends discovered by Pinker "are not subtle—many of the changes involve an order of magnitude or more. Even when his explanations do not fully convince, they are serious and well-grounded."[3]

While many academics agree that Pinker's numbers show a downward trend in violence, critics tend to disagree with the explanations for it.[4] For example, the American academic Bradley A. Thayer* thinks that the decline is more plausibly due to power balances in the West, and argues that it is more fragile than Pinker thinks.[5] Others say that Pinker does not give enough weight to material and institutional factors, as opposed to cultural ones.[6]

Pinker's critics can be divided into two groups: the first questions the book's conceptual foundations; the second underlines the shortcomings of its data.

The dispute with this second group is methodological: where and how can data on mortality be gathered, and how should it be interpreted? The Lebanese American statistician Nassim Nicholas Taleb* points to some fallacies in Pinker's statistical analysis,[7] stating that his "estimation from past data has monstrous errors. A record of the people who died in the last few years has very very little predictive powers of how many will die the next year, and is biased downward. One biological event can decimate the population."[8] The Australian academic Jeff Lewis,* meanwhile, accuses Pinker of relying on a very small dataset and points out that the exclusion of after-war mortality data is problematic.

> "Steven Pinker's The Better Angels of Our Nature: Why Violence Has Declined stands out as one of the most important books I've read—not just this year, but ever ... The book is about violence, but paints a remarkable picture that shows the world has evolved over time to be a far less violent place than before. It offers a really fresh perspective on how to achieve positive outcomes in the world."
>
> —— Bill Gates, *My Bookshelf*

Responses

The critics who question Pinker's conceptual approach in *The Better Angels* include the British political philosopher John Gray* and the American journalist Elizabeth Kolbert.* Gray says that Pinker is wrong in thinking that science and humanism* belong together. Referencing the broad legacy of the nineteenth-century naturalist Charles Darwin,* a pioneering figure in the history of evolutionary science* and the rational social philosophy of humanism,* Gray writes,"Science and humanism are at odds more often than they are at one. For a devoted Darwinist like Pinker to maintain that the world is being pacified by the spread of a particular world view is deeply ironic. There is nothing in Darwinism to suggest that ideas and beliefs can transform human life."[9]

In the same vein, Elizabeth Kolbert observes that the very forces that produced Pinker's moral progress were also responsible for some of history's worst atrocities.

In response, Pinker restates his position: [10] he does not claim that the world feels less dangerous, but he claims that it is—objectively—less violent.[11] He claims that Taleb seems to misunderstand the whole project of The Better Angels: that it is descriptive, not predictive,[12] and that he is not trying to present a prediction about violence in the future.[13] The problem outlined by Taleb is not, therefore, relevant to the book's interpretation of why violence has declined.

Against critics such as Lewis, Pinker remarks that they focus only on specific examples in his data, and do not look at the whole picture. Even if some of the data is indeed imprecise, the global picture still shows a decline in violence.

These discussions have not resulted in major revisions to the work. They have, however, forced Pinker to return to his claims and support them with more data.

Conflict and Consensus

Despite the popularity of *The Better Angels*, there is very little agreement about the major claims of the book, and many of its critics remain unconvinced. But Pinker's data on the trends of violence have been the subject of a consensus. Indeed, a 2012 document from the Human Security Report Project* discusses Pinker's book and concludes, "Today there is broad agreement within the research community that the number and deadliness of interstate wars has declined dramatically."[14]

Pinker was not the first to show that there has been a decline in violence over the centuries. As a result, it is not clear whether this consensus about it was reached thanks to him, or if was already present in some fields, such as history and criminology* (a field of research concerned with the exploration, understanding, and prevention of criminal behavior in individuals and societies). Either way, Pinker presents original data that had not been compiled before. From this point of view he contributed original research to the debate.

Following the attack by terrorists on the French satirical magazine *Charlie Hebdo** in Paris and the ongoing conflict in Syria,* Pinker has returned to his proposal. Referencing the long period of global tension known as the Cold War,* which ended in 1991 with the final collapse of Soviet Union,* Pinker published an article in September 2015 in the British *Guardian* newspaper in which he argued, "I put my optimism on trial by updating my graphs ... Discouragingly, the precipitous decline in the number of civil wars after the end of the cold war, from 26 in 1992 to four in 2007, has bent back up to 11 in 2014 ... One of these wars, in Syria, also caused a small bounce in the global rate of war deaths after a vertiginous six-decade plunge ... The good news is that this is the only bad news: the rate of every other kind of violence has stuck to its recent low or declined even further."[15]

---

1. A list of reviews can be found at Cognitive Science Perspectives on Conflict, Violence, Peace and Justice (course outline), accessed December 30, 2015, http://web.stanford.edu/class/symsys203/.

2. Peter Singer, "Is Violence History?" *New York Times*, October 6, 2011, accessed December 30, 2015, http://www.nytimes.com/2011/10/09/books/review/the-better-angels-of-our-nature-by-steven-pinker-book-review. html.

3. Robert Jervis, "Pinker the Prophet," *National Interest*, Nov—Dec 2011, accessed December 30, 2015, http://nationalinterest.org/bookreview/pinker-the-prophet-6072.

4. Nils Petter Gleditsch et al., "The Forum: The Decline of War," *International Studies Review* 15, no. 3 (2013): 396–419.

5. Bradley A. Thayer, "Humans, not Angels: Reasons to Doubt the Decline of War Thesis," in "The Forum: The Decline of War," *International Studies Review* 15, no. 3 (2013): 407.

6. Jack S. Levy and William R. Thompson, "The Decline of War: Multiple Trajectories and Diverging Trends," in "The Forum: The Decline of War," *International Studies Review* 15, no. 3 (2013): 412.

7. Nassim Nicholas Taleb, "The 'Long Peace' is a Statistical Illusion," accessed December 30, 2015, http://www.fooledbyrandomness.com/longpeace.pdf.

8. Nassim Nicholas Taleb, Facebook, accessed December 30, 2015, https: //www.facebook.com/permalink.php?story_fbid=10151641931853375& id=13012333374.

9. John Gray, "Delusions of Peace," *Prospect*, September 21, 2011, accessed December 30, 2015, http://www.prospectmagazine.co.uk/features/john-gray-steven-pinker-violence-review.

10. For the debate, see John Gray, "John Gray: Steven Pinker is wrong about violence and war," *Guardian*, March 13, 2015, accessed December 30, 2015, http://www.theguardian.com/books/2015/mar/13/john-gray-steven-pinker-wrong-violence-war-declining.

11. Steven Pinker, "Frequently Asked Questions about *The Better Angels of Our Nature: Why Violence*

Has Declined," accessed December 30, 2015, http://stevenpinker.com/pages/frequently-asked-questions-about-better-angels-our-nature-why-violence-has-declined.

12. Steven Pinker, "Fooled by Belligerence. Comments on Nassim Taleb's 'The Long Peace is a Statistical Illusion,'" accessed December 30, 2015, http://stevenpinker.com/files/comments_on_taleb_by_s_pinker.pdf.

13. Pinker, "Fooled by Belligerence."

14. HSRP, "The Decline in Global Violence: Reality or Myth?" March 3, 2014, accessed December 29, 2015, http://www.hsrgroup.org/docs/Publications/HSR2013/HSR_2013_Press_Release.pdf.

15. Steven Pinker, "Now For The Good News: Things Really Are Getting Better," *Guardian*, September 11, 2015, accessed December 19, 2015, http://www. theguardian.com/commentisfree/2015/sep/11/news-isis-syria-headlines-violence-steven-pinker.

THE EVOLVING DEBATE

KEY POINTS

* *The Better Angels* offers (to date) the most comprehensive data in support of the claim that violence is declining.

* While we cannot talk about a "school of thought" emerging from *The Better Angels*, a broad group of thinkers and public figures have been inspired by the text.

* The book has influenced not only members of the academic world, but also entrepreneurs such as the American cofounder of Microsoft, Bill Gates,* and the American cofounder of Facebook, Mark Zuckerberg.*

Uses and Problems

Steven Pinker's *The Better Angels of Our Nature: Why Violence Has Declined* was published in 2011. It is therefore too early to chart its influence on other authors. Nonetheless, we can gauge how this influence may develop in the uses made of the text in the years since its publication. Several studies on trends of violence cite the text.[1] The 2014 special volume of the peer-reviewed journal *Evolutionary Psychology* focuses on the evolution of violence and makes many references to *The Better Angels*.[2] Across a wide range of disciplines in the social sciences, readers have responded to *The Better Angels* by modifying, completing, and criticizing some of its shortcomings.

For example, in a publication of 2015, historians and sociologists working on the history of crime assessed the decline of homicide in 55 countries since 1950. They found that the downward trend in violence has been widespread.[3] They refer to Pinker's work in the paper, but contrary to the proposal of *The Better Angels* they did not find a strong connection between the decline of violence and modernization* (the process of the transformation of societies from preindustrial, traditional, agrarian, and religious to fully industrial, urban, and secular). While all 55 countries showed signs of declining violence, only rich and Western-style democracies* showed this connection. They concluded with a more modest take on Pinker's thesis: "The view that violent crimes are on the decline because modernization is transforming the world ... is an exceedingly broad one. Our study is limited to a single type of violence, over a 60-year time frame, and based on an examination of a non-random sample of mostly wealthy Western-style democracies. For this highly select undertaking, high modernization does not provide a complete explanation and yet such a view fits the data better than a conflict view."[4]

> "In April 2012, we invited dozens of scholars from around the USA to join us at Oakland University in Rochester, Michigan for a day-long interdisciplinary conference on 'The Evolution of Violence.'This conference followed a visit and lecture the day before by Steven Pinker on his recent book, The Better Angels of Our Nature. We invited as panelists some of the leading violence scholars from many different disciplines, including psychology, criminology, biology, anthropology, archeology, law, philosophy, and medicine."
>
> ——Todd K. Shackelford and Ranald D. Hansen,
> *Preface to The Evolution of Violence*

Schools of Thought

There are two principle reasons why *The Better Angels* has yet to create a school of thought. One is that it was published very recently and it is too early to assess its long-term influence. The other is that the scope of the book is broad and encompasses many disciplines. As a result, it might be having an influence without creating a cohesive set of thinkers who identify explicitly with the ideas presented in the book.

The Better Angels has a place within a general world view that can be broadly defined as optimistic about the progress of humanity. According to Pinker, thinkers and philosophers who have taken this view include the French philosopher Auguste Comte,* the English philosophers John Stuart Mill,* Thomas Hobbes,* and John Locke,* the Scottish economist* David Hume,* and the German philosopher* Immanuel Kant.* And the book appeals to many thinkers from different areas, both inside and outside academia. The American technologists and philanthropists Bill Gates and Mark Zuckerberg both admire the text, as do prominent academics including the Australian philosopher Peter Singer* and the British political scientist* Adam Roberts.*[5] Singer declared it a "supremely important book."[6] The book, for them, gives hope for real progress (maybe a moral progress in Singer's case) in history.

In Current Scholarship

So far no clear disciple or successor has emerged who shares

The Better Angels' overall project. There are, however, many researchers who use the work as a starting point for their scientific inquiries. In the field of anthropology,* several researchers are investigating the biological and cultural origins of violence. They are using Pinker's book either to develop his proposals in more detail, or as a negative starting point. For example, some have accepted his claim that violence declines as people move from hunter-gatherer* societies to societies organized along the lines of a state.[7] Others oppose this view; for them, hunter-gatherer societies are not considerably more violent than state societies.*[8] Like Pinker, they base their claims on data and on available evidence.

Another example of the use of *The Better Angels* in current scholarship is in evolutionary psychology.* Here the book forms the starting point for a debate about the biological origins of violence; the editors of a special volume on the evolution of violence acknowledge their debt to the work.[9] A final example is in international politics, which has also referenced *The Better Angels* in discussions. In 2013, the peer-reviewed journal *International Studies Review* carried a piece stating that "several authors have announced a 'waning of war' in recent decades (including a cognitive psychologist with a massive 800-page tome (Pinker 2011))." It continues, "Despite the breadth of this literature, this is not the end of the argument, but rather the start of a long debate."[10]

1. Timothy Kohler et al., "The Better Angels of Their Nature: Declining Violence Through Time Among Prehispanic Farmers of the Pueblo Southwest," *American Antiquity* 79, no. 3 (2014): 444–64.

2. Todd Kennedy Shackelford and Ranald D. Hansen, *The Evolution of Violence* (New York: Springer Verlag, 2014).

3. Gary LaFree et al., "How Effective Are Our 'Better Angels'? Assessing Country-level Declines in Homicide Since 1950," *European Journal of Criminology* 12, no. 4 (2015): 482–504.

4. LaFree et al., "How Effective Are Our 'Better Angels'?," 495.

5. Adam Roberts, "The Long Peace Getting Longer," *Survival* 54, no. 1 (2012): 175–83.

6. Peter Singer, "Is Violence History?" *New York Times*, October 6, 2011, accessed December 30, 2015, http://www.nytimes.com/2011/10/09/books/review/the-better-angels-of-our-nature-by-steven-pinker-book-review. html.

7. Nam C. Kim, "Angels, Illusions, Hydras, and Chimeras: Violence and Humanity," *Reviews in Anthropology* 41, no. 4 (2012): 239–72.

8. Geoffrey Benjamin et al., "Violence: Finding Peace," *Science* 338, no. 6105 (2012): 327.

9. Shackelford and Hansen, *The Evolution of Violence.*

10. Nils Petter Gleditsch et al."The Forum: The Decline of War," *International Studies Review* 15, no. 3 (2013): 396-419

MODULE 11
IMPACT AND INFLUENCE TODAY

KEY POINTS

* *The Better Angels* is still at the center of debates on the history and origins of violence.

* Pinker's book continues to challenge the received view that the present is the most violent era in human history.

* Critics of the book take a broadly negative world view of humanity and its future.

Position

Steven Pinker's book *The Better Angels of Our Nature: Why Violence Has Declined* defends the optimistic idea that violence has been steadily declining over the course of history. The book's central claims are still discussed and cited. His ideas have been referenced in recent work on morality and empathy,*[1] and used to explore the trends of violence in new geographical areas and at different moments in history.[2] The text is also referenced in current debates about violence.[3]

One area in which the book contributes to ongoing debates concerns the relation between violence and climate change.* Pinker mentions global warming,* but he suggests that it will not have a significant impact on levels of violence. His argument is that conflicts are more likely to occur in poor and politically unstable countries than in countries that suffer natural disasters, "since the state of the environment is at most one ingredient in a mixture that depends far more on political and social organization, [wars over resources] are far from inevitable, even in a climate-changed world."[4] Pinker reasons that strongly democratic* and wealthy countries can react promptly to natural disasters and contain their consequences. This helps them avoid the possibly violent ramifications of these events.

The book has revived interest in the study of statistical trends related to violence and in the study of factors that trigger (or limit) violence. The current consensus is that *The Better Angels* is a key reference book for any discussion of these issues. It is, though, too early to say whether this trend will continue.

> *"The Better Angels of Our Nature is a supremely important book … But what of the future? Our improved understanding of violence, of which Pinker's book is an example, can be a valuable tool to maintain peace and reduce crime, but other factors are in play."*
>
> ——Peter Singer, *Is Violence History?*

Interaction

Drawing on the aims and methods of different academic fields, *The Better Angels* is an interdisciplinary work. Pinker's inspiration came partly from his desire to challenge the idea, widespread in the social sciences,* that humans are blank slates. To those who subscribe to this belief, there are no innate biological or psychological* faculties: everything comes from society and culture (an idea Pinker attributes to the followers of the influential German American anthropologist* Franz Boas).*[5] If this is true, violence cannot be a biological phenomenon; it is merely societal and cultural. Pinker challenges this view and argues that people have some innate predispositions toward violence. He also suggests that these may, to some degree, be tamed through historical processes.

The Better Angels also challenges the view that violence is rising. These challenges have sparked an immediate response: for example, the British philosopher* John Gray* reacted to Pinker's underlying conceptions of human nature and history. Gray expresses a negative, pessimistic view of human nature and adopts a broadly Hobbesian* world view; the seventeenth-century English philosopher Thomas Hobbes argued that humans are selfish and self-serving, and that without a powerful government to hold these impulses in check, we live in a state of perpetual conflict. Gray's opinions of humanity and its future are radically different to those of Pinker. It is unsurprising, then, that there are differences between them on the subject of human violence.

The Continuing Debate

The debate between Pinker and his opponents is less about Pinker's text than about differences in ideas, world views, and conceptions of humanity. Such debates are not easily settled. In writing *The Better Angels*, Pinker was opposing several schools of thought. One is a school of anthropology that Pinker calls "anthropologists for peace," which, he claims, is driven by an agenda: it wants to show that non-state* societies are peaceful. In contrast, Pinker does not want to prove that humans are either naturally peaceful or naturally violent. He paints a nuanced picture: humans can be either peaceful or violent, depending on their circumstances. It is, however, a crucial element of his argument that state-based societies help promote a decrease in violence. Responding to Pinker, these anthropologists assert that their aim is not ideological,* but empirical.*[6]

Another example of a hard-to-resolve debate is the one between Pinker and John Gray. He believes that Pinker's vision of the future is determined by his blind faith in science and lacks a deeper understanding of human nature. Gray's view is that "peace and freedom alternate with war and tyranny ... Instead of becoming ever stronger and more widely spread, civilization remains inherently fragile and regularly succumbs to barbarism."[7] Pinker replies by pointing out the ideological disagreement between them: "As a part of his [Gray's] campaign against reason, science and Enlightenment humanism, he insists that the strivings of humanity over the centuries have left us no better off."[8] His response to Gray's challenge is to highlight his statistical evidence that shows a decline in violence.

---

1. Jean Decety and Jason M. Cowell, "The Complex Relation Between Morality and Empathy," *Trends in Cognitive Sciences* 18, no. 7 (2014): 337–9.

2. Timothy Kohler et al., "The Better Angels of Their Nature: Declining Violence Through Time Among Prehispanic Farmers of the Pueblo Southwest," *American Antiquity* 79, no. 3 (2014): 444–64.

3. Steven Pinker, "Now For The Good News: Things Really Are Getting Better," *Guardian*, September 11, 2015, accessed December 19, 2015, http://www.theguardian.com/commentisfree/2015/sep/11/news-isis-syria-headlines-violence-steven-pinker.

4. Steven Pinker, *The Better Angels of Our Nature: Why Violence Has Declined* (London: Penguin,

2011), 377.

5. Steven Pinker, *The Blank Slate: the Modern Denial of Human Nature* (London: Penguin, 2002), 36.

6. Geoffrey Benjamin et al., "Violence: Finding Peace," *Science* 338, no. 6105 (2012): 327.

7. John Gray, "Steven Pinker is wrong about violence and war," *Guardian*, March 13, 2015, accessed December 30, 2015, http://www.theguardian. com/books/2015/mar/13/john-gray-steven-pinker-wrong-violence-war-declining.

8. Steven Pinker, "Guess what? More people are living in peace now. Just look at the numbers," *Guardian*, March 20, 2015, accessed December 30, 2015, http://www.theguardian.com/commentisfree/2015/mar/20/wars-john-gray-conflict-peace.

WHERE NEXT?

KEY POINTS

* *The Better Angels* is likely to remain a reference point for future studies on violence.

* Its impact is likely to be on research into the connections between the history and psychology* of violence.

* *The Better Angels* may also have an impact on the field of developmental psychology* (the study of the infant mind and how psychological faculties develop over time from birth to adulthood). Pinker suggests studying the evolution of violent psychology by looking at the context in which a person grows up.

Potential

Steven Pinker's book *The Better Angels of Our Nature: How Violence Has Declined* has the potential to be at the center of future debates on the history, sociology* and psychology of violence. It introduces a bold thesis about violence and a clear methodology to support it.

Pinker's data shows that violence is declining. One of the book's strengths is that its arguments are founded on evidence. But new data may emerge to show that violence is increasing, contradicting Pinker's ideas. In an article published on September 11, 2015, Pinker looks at the new trends and claims that they still support his thesis: "The most concentrated forms of destruction our sorry species has dreamed up are world war and nuclear war, and we have extended our streak of avoiding them to 70 years. Wars between great powers, also hugely destructive, have been absent for almost as long—62 years."[1]

The book is largely descriptive: it presents historical trends and psychological explanations for violence. While Pinker does not attempt to give instructions as to how violence can be controlled and reduced, the connection he draws between psychology and society plays an important role in his overall argument. These ideas may have a particular impact on the educational sphere, and the ways in which pacifism* and cooperation can be taught.

> "But headlines are a poor guide to history. People's sense of danger is warped by the availability of memorable examples— which is why we are more afraid of getting eaten by a shark than falling down the stairs, though the latter is more likely to kill us. Peaceful territories, no matter how numerous, don't make news, and people quickly forget the wars and atrocities of even the recent past."
> ——Steven Pinker, "Now For The Good News: Things Really Are Getting Better"

Future Directions

Although *The Better Angels* aims to connect psychology with history, the section of the book that dwells on psychology is shorter than Pinker's historical overview of violence. It is clear that more research is needed to discover how psychology is shaped by the historical context. Pinker mentions a model from cognitive anthropology* that argues that there are universal ways in which social relations are established and understood. These are the "relational models" developed by the American anthropologist Alan Fiske.* But the detail about how cognitive anthropology, psychology, and society are linked is not clear. There is work to be done on the evolutionary* aspects of conflict and of cooperation. This would give substance to the explanatory part of the book.

The book offers a starting point for both evolutionary psychologists* and developmental psychologists interested in discovering the origins of violence. Sociologists and historians interested in the book's major thesis are likely to look at the data it is based upon, and carefully analyze historical trends to confirm or refute it.

Another area in which Pinker's ideas may be applied is in the field of technology.Mark Zuckerberg,* the American founder of Facebook, has asked Pinker whether any data exists about the role of the Internet in reducing violence. Pinker has replied that new technologies play a role in the propagation of cosmopolitanism* (the belief that human beings form a single community) and that cosmopolitanism has a positive impact on violence.[2]

While Pinker might not have a group of disciples or students working on the topic of *The Better Angels*, he is surrounded by sympathetic colleagues, such as the Australian philosopher* Peter Singer* and the British evolutionary psychologist Richard Dawkins.* They are likely to carry on reflecting on the issues explored in the book.

Summary

Violence is a central characteristic of human history and psychology. *The Better Angels* connects these two areas in a comprehensive study of the history of violence and its psychological roots. This ambitious book is one of Pinker's best sellers and the one that has sparked the most animated debate, both in the academic sphere and more widely. These debates are likely to continue.

Previous studies of violence have focused either on its history or on the psychology that underlies violent behavior, but few have brought these aspects together. In addition, most studies of violence have tended to view humanity in a polarized manner: either as originally good, but perverted by society, which has made it violent; or originally evil, and incapable of being changed by society. *The Better Angels* is not founded on either of these views. Pinker tries to show the ways in which nature and nurture* interact: while human biology is in many ways inflexible, society and culture can influence our behavior.

The Better Angels is an appealing book because it is positive about the future of humanity. Its thesis is supported by data and statistical analysis; it is not based on naïve optimism. The work is challenging, because its optimism contrasts with many people's intuitive view of the world as increasingly dangerous and threatening. It has become prominent, in part, because of its capacity to prompt a lively debate about one of the most central aspects of human nature: violence.

1. Steven Pinker, "Now For The Good News: Things Really Are Getting Better," *Guardian*, September 11, 2015, accessed December 30, 2015, http://www.theguardian.com/commentisfree/2015/sep/11/news-isis-syria-headlines-violence-steven-pinker.

2. Mark Zuckerberg, "A Year of Books," Facebook, January 28, 2015, accessed December 30, 2015, https: //www.facebook.com/ayearofbooks/posts/831583243554273.

GLOSSARY OF TERMS

1. **Anarchism:** a theory in political philosophy that promotes eliminating the state and establishing self-governing, free societies. There are many strands of anarchism but they are all identified by the rejection of institutionalized political power. One of the main anarchist thinkers was the Russian revolutionary Mikhail Bakunin.

2. **Anthropology:** the study of humans. It concerns the study of all aspects of humanity: biological, linguistic, social, and cultural. It belongs to the field of social science.

3. **Archeology:** a discipline that studies human life and activity in the past by exploring artifacts, architecture, and cultural landscapes (a combination of natural and man-made works). It belongs to the field of social science.

4. **Atheism:** the position that there are no deities or gods.

5. **Biology:** a field of study that belongs to the natural sciences and is concerned with the exploration of living organisms: their development, structure, function, classification, and distribution.

6. *Charlie Hebdo* **attack:** the killing and injury of the members of the French satirical weekly newspaper *Charlie Hebdo*. It was carried out on January 7, 2015 by two gunmen who declared they were members of an al-Qaeda branch inYemen.

7. **Christianity:** a monotheistic Abrahamic religion whose major text is the New Testament. The core belief of Christianity is that Jesus Christ is the Messiah, the savior of humanity, and was foreseen in the Old Testament.

8. **Civilizing process:** a term used by Steven Pinker and borrowed from the German-born sociologist Norbert Elias. The term indicates a set of institutional changes that began during the Middle Ages, and had an impact on human psychology that helped lead to a reduction in human violence.

9. **Climate change:** long-lasting changes in weather patterns. Climate change is mostly measured by archeological evidence, temperature measurements, and changes in vegetal and animal presence.

10. **Cognition:** used in a restricted sense, this refers to the mental faculties involved

in post-perceptual processing, such as memory, judgment, decision-making, and language. Used in a broader sense, cognition refers to all mental processes, including perception, memory, attention, language, decision-making, reasoning, judgment, and problem-solving.

11. **Cognitive anthropology:** an approach to the study of anthropology that draws on the aims and methods of cognitive science.

12. **Cognitive science:** the interdisciplinary study of the mind and brain. It draws on philosophy, psychology, neuroscience, artificial intelligence, linguistics, and anthropology. Its core hypothesis is that the mind and the brain are representational-computational devices, similar in some respects to computers, and that we can study them by using experimental methods.

13. **Cold War:** a period of political and military tension between the Western Bloc (the United States and its allies) and the Eastern Bloc (the Soviet Union and its allies) that lasted from 1947 to 1991. It is called "cold" because it never resulted in direct conflict between the United States and the Soviet Union, but was conducted in satellite countries and mostly concerned the relative distribution of power.

14. **Collectivist anarchism:** a political theory that argued for the abolition of the state, and for the tools and resources required for production to be collectively owned.

15. **Colonialism:** the exploitation and government of a territory by a power from another territory.

16. **Cosmopolitanism:** the belief that all human beings are citizens of a single community. According to Steven Pinker, cosmopolitanism is one of the cultural forces that can help to reduce violence.

17. **Criminology:** an interdisciplinary field of research concerned with the exploration, understanding, and prevention of criminal behavior in individuals and societies.

18. **Crusades:** a series of wars fought between the eleventh and the thirteenth centuries. The first Crusade took place in 1095 when an army of Western

European Christians set out to fight against Muslim forces and reconquer the Holy Land (the region located between the River Jordan and the Mediterranean).

19. **Darwinism:** a set of ideas associated with the English naturalist Charles Darwin and his theory of evolution.

20. **Democracy:** a system of government in which the people freely elect their representatives.

21. **Developmental psychology:** the study of the infant mind and the development of psychological faculties over time from birth to adulthood.

22. **Domestic violence:** the use of physical and psychological violence in the context of a family or home, usually by a partner.

23. **Economics:** an academic discipline that studies economic systems — the production, trade, and consumption of goods (material and non-material, such as services).

24. **Empathy:** the capacity to understand the situation, experiences, and feelings of others from their perspective rather than one's own.

25. **Empirical:** this term is usually applied to knowledge. It indicates knowledge acquired through observation and experiments rather than through mere reflection and theorizing.

26. **Empiricism:** a philosophical school of thought according to which knowledge comes from experience and that there are no innate bodies of knowledge. Associated with the philosophers John Locke, David Hume, and Thomas Hobbes. Also present in psychology.

27. **Enlightenment:** an intellectual movement that appeared in the eighteenth century in Europe (and partially in the United States), characterized by the appeal to rationality and the defense of liberty, tolerance, and rights.

28. **Equity feminism:** equity feminists are mostly interested in legal equality (for example, women receiving the same salary as men for doing the same work) and are neutral on the issue of gender roles. Gender feminists have a broader outlook and are often associated with the idea that gender roles are a social construction.

29. **Ethnography:** the study of people's cultures, particularly by observing them from the inside.

30. **Eurozone:** the monetary union of 19 member states of the European Union (while there are 28 EU states in total, 9 are not part of the Eurozone). These states have adopted the euro as their shared currency.

31. **Evolution:** processes occurring by means of changes in the heritable traits in a given biological population over time and generations.

32. **Evolutionary psychology:** the study of human and nonhuman psychology from the perspective of modern evolutionary theory.

33. **Expanding circle:** a concept proposed by the Australian moral philosopher Peter Singer. Singer says there is a moral progress as our moral concerns extend to beings that are not closely related to us. This connects with Steven Pinker's discussion of empathy as one of the psychological mechanisms that reduces violence.

34. **Experimental psychology:** the study of the human mind and behavior via methods that aim for measurable results that have a degree of scientific accuracy.

35. **Feminism:** a movement whose goal is to achieve equal rights for women and, more generally, to advocate for women in society, politics, and culture.

36. **Gender:** a set of characteristics broadly related to the difference between masculinity and femininity. Gender differences are not only biological, unlike sex differences.

37. **Genocide:** the systematic elimination of a group based on racial, ethnic, religious, cultural, or national features.

38. **Global warming:** a gradual increase in the average temperature of the earth due to human influence on the climate and environment.

39. **Humanism:** a set of rational principles in which supreme importance is placed on humanity rather than on religious or "divine" institutions or figures.

40. **Human rights:** the most general set of rights to which humans are entitled, simply by virtue of being human: for example, freedom from torture.

41. **Human Security Report Project:** a research project studying peace and conflict, based in Canada. Its aim is to examine long-term trends in violent conflicts.

42. **Hunter-gatherer:** people who lived by hunting and collecting rather than developing agriculture.

43. **Ideology:** a system of norms, beliefs, and theories held by a group or by individuals.

44. **Inquisition:** an institution established by the Christian Church in the thirteenth century to ensure the purity of belief and religious practice. Later it was notorious for the use of torture in the extraction of confessions.

45. **Leviathan:** a mythical monster in the Old Testament. The expression was used by the English philosopher Thomas Hobbes to indicate an absolute sovereign.

46. **Linguistics:** a discipline concerned with the study of language and its different aspects.

47. **Medieval:** relating to the Middle Ages (fifth to fifteenth century).

48. **Middle Ages:** a period of European history between the fifth century (the decline of the Western Roman Empire) and the fifteenth century (the beginning of the period of European history known as the Renaissance).

49. **Modernization:** the process whereby societies are transformed from pre-industrial, traditional, agrarian, and religious to fully industrial, urban, and secular.

50. **Moral philosophy:** inquiry into the nature of "right behavior" and ethics.

51. **Nativist:** in the context of psychology, a nativist thinker believes that certain things are "native" to the human mind—in other words, we are born with them.

52. **Nature and nurture:** sometimes "nature versus nurture," the phrase indicates the opposition between two forces that influence development: "nature" refers to innate, biological factors, while "nurture" indicates external, environmental (including cultural and social) factors.

53. **Nazism:** a political and ideological set of ideas associated with the Nazi Party of

Germany in the 1930s and 1940s.

54. **Noble savage:** an expression that indicates a hypothetical indigenous person who has not been corrupted and perverted by civilization. The term comes from Dryden's play *The Conquest of Granada* (1672). Often used in relation to Rousseau's theory that the "state of nature," or the natural human state, is peaceful.

55. **Non-state societies:** societies living without a stable state or authority. Examples of non-state societies are bands, tribes, and chiefdoms. Such societies were more widespread in the pre-historic era (around 10,000 b.c.e.), but this is now a marginal way of living.

56. **Normative:** pertaining to norms and rules for guiding behavior.

57. **Pacifism:** the refusal to sanction war, violence, and militarism.

58. **Philosophy:** a systematic study of the most fundamental nature of reality.

59. **Policy analysis/analyst:** the study and evaluation of policies and programs and their implications, aimed at solving public problems; a political analyst is one who engages in this study.

60. **Political science:** the study of politics and how governments or political institutions work and behave, from a wide range of perspectives.

61. **Prescriptive:** related to guidelines and rules aimed at reinforcing certain kinds of behaviors.

62. **Psychology:** the scientific study of the mind and the behavior of groups and individuals. Psychology explores how mental functions, such as perception, memory, and decision-making, work. The subject belongs to the social sciences. In a general sense, the terms "psychology" and "psychological" refer to the workings of the mind.

63. **Pugnacity:** the tendency to be aggressive or pugnacious.

64. **Scientific method:** a set of steps used in science to investigate the world. It involves the careful formulation of a hypothesis and methods for testing that hypothesis.

65. **Secular:** not connected to religion; exempt from religious rules.

66. **Sociology:** the study of society. Examples of topics studied by sociologists are religion, politics, and social class. One of the social sciences.

67. **Social sciences:** a wide field of academic investigation that includes anthropology, archaeology, demography, economics, history, human geography, international relations, law, linguistics, political science, pedagogy, and psychology.

68. **State of nature:** a concept in political philosophy that indicated the hypothetical lives of people before the rise of societies and states.

69. **Syrian conflict:** an ongoing conflict that started in 2011 in Syria. It began with demonstrations against the government of the Syrian president, Bashar al-Assad, with protesters demanding his resignation. It continues to this day.

70. **Terrorism:** acts aimed at provoking terror, often with the purpose of having a political impact.

71. **Testosterone:** a hormone present in both nonhuman and human animals that is secreted mostly by testicles in human males and, in minor quantities, by ovaries in human females. Usually associated with masculine traits.

72. **Ukrainian conflict:** an ongoing conflict that started in 2013 in Donetsk, Ukraine, between pro-and anti-Russian groups. Donetsk is an area of Ukraine in which the majority of the population speaks Russian.

73. **Uppsala Conflict Data Project:** a program founded in the 1970s and hosted at the University of Uppsala, Sweden. Its aim is to collect data on violent conflicts around the world.

74. **Women's rights:** rights aimed at promoting women's equality with men.

75. **World War:** a war involving most of the world's countries. The term refers to two events of the twentieth century: World War I (1914–18) and World War II (1939–45).

1. **Mikhail Bakunin (1814−76)** was a Russian revolutionary thinker, best known as one of the founders of the anarchist movement.

2. **Franz Boas (1858−1942)** was a German American thinker, considered one of the founders of modern anthropology. He taught at Columbia University where he established a school. One of his major texts is *The Mind of Primitive Men*, published in 1911.

3. **Noam Chomsky (b. 1928)** is an American linguist, cognitive scientist, and political activist. Professor emeritus at MIT, he is best known for his theory of "generative grammar." Steven Pinker helped bring his ideas on language to the broader public.

4. **Gregory Clark (b. 1957)** is an economic historian who specializes in the wealth of nations.

5. **Roger Cohen (b. 1955)** is an English journalist who writes for *the New York Times* and *the International New York Times*.

6. **Auguste Comte (1798−1857)** was a French philosopher and one of the founders of positivism, a philosophical movement based on the idea that all knowledge should be modeled on the example of scientific knowledge. He is considered one of the founders of sociology.

7. **Leda Cosmides (b. 1957)** is an American psychologist, best known as one of the founders of evolutionary psychology.

8. **John Crawfurd (1783−1868)** was a Scottish diplomat whose work anticipated ethnological studies.

9. **Martin Daly (b. 1944)** is a Canadian evolutionary psychologist.

10. **Charles Darwin (1809−82)** was an English naturalist, best known for his groundbreaking work on the theory of evolution in *On the Origin of Species* (1859).

11. **Richard Dawkins (b. 1941)** is a British ethologist (someone engaged in the study of animal behavior) and evolutionary psychologist, currently an emeritus

fellow of New College in Oxford. He is best known for his 1976 book *The Selfish Gene*, which presents a gene-centered theory of evolution.

12. **David Deutsch (b. 1953)** is a British physicist at Oxford University; he also writes about creativity and the history of knowledge.

13. **Jared Diamond (b. 1937)** is an American scientist and professor of geography at the University of California, working in anthropology and evolutionary biology, among other fields.

14. **Norbert Elias (1897 – 1990)** was a German British sociologist, author of *The Civilizing Process* (published in German in 1939 and translated into English in 1969). This book examines how manners have changed over time and how these changes have had an impact on human psychology.

15. **Alan Fiske (b. 1947)** is an American anthropologist at the University of California who works on the anthropology and psychology of human relationships. He is best known for his theory of "social relational models."

16. **Bill Gates (b. 1955)** is an American entrepreneur, computer programmer, and philanthropist, best known as the cofounder of software company Microsoft.

17. **Joshua Goldstein (b. 1952)** is an American professor emeritus of international relations at the American University in Washington, DC; he specializes in war and society.

18. **Rebecca Goldstein (b. 1950)** is an American novelist, best known for her novel *The Mind—Body Problem*. She is Steven Pinker's third wife.

19. **John Gray (b. 1948)** is an English political philosopher and frequent contributor to newspapers such as *the Guardian* and *the Times Literary Supplement*. His most famous books are *Straw Dogs: Thoughts on Humans and Other Animals* (2003) and *Black Mass: Apocalyptic Religion and the Death of Utopia* (2007), in which he expresses a pessimistic outlook on humanity.

20. **Ted Robert Gurr (b. 1936)** is an American political scientist working on issues concerning political conflict. He is now professor emeritus at the University of Maryland.

21. **Ranald D. Hansen (d. 2014)** was a professor of psychology at Oakland University, specializing in the evolutionary psychology of violence and sexuality.

22. **Thomas Hobbes (1588 – 1679)** was an English philosopher who worked on a variety of topics, but is now best known for his political philosophy. His most famous book is *Leviathan* (1651).

23. **David Hume (1711 – 76)** was a Scottish philosopher and one of the major figures of the empiricist and skeptic tradition. His best-known work is *A Treatise of Human Nature* (1739–40).

24. **Robert Jervis (b. 1940)** is a professor of international affairs at Columbia University.

25. **Immanuel Kant (1724 – 1804)** was a German philosopher who worked on all areas of knowledge. His three Critiques are some of the most important works in the history of philosophy.

26. **Elizabeth Kolbert (b. 1961)** is an American journalist and contributor to the *New Yorker*.

27. **Stephen Kosslyn (b. 1948)** is an American psychologist and neuroscientist, best known for his work on mental imagery and information processing. He was Steven Pinker's advisor at Harvard University.

28. **Jeff Lewis** is a professor of media and cultural studies at the RMIT University in Melbourne, Australia who has produced influential work on violence and terrorism.

29. **Abraham Lincoln (1809 – 65)** was the 16th president of the United States, in office during the American Civil War and assassinated just after the war ended.

30. **John Locke (1632 – 1704)** was an English philosopher in the empiricist tradition, mostly known for his conception of the mind and for his political philosophy.

31. **John Stuart Mill (1806 – 73)** was a British philosopher, economist, and political thinker and one of the main representatives of utilitarianism. His

principal works were *On Liberty* and *Utilitarianism*.

32. **Robert Muchembled (b. 1944)** is a French historian who specializes in the history of violence; he is also interested in the history of sexuality. In 2011 he published the English translation of his book *A History of Violence: From the End of the Middle Ages to the Present.*

33. **Lewis Fry Richardson (1881 – 1953)** was an English mathematician, best known for his work on meteorology. He was one of the first thinkers to apply mathematical and statistical techniques to the study of the causes of wars and conflicts.

34. **Adam Roberts (b. 1940)** is an English professor of international relations at Oxford University, best known for his work on international security, organization, law, and civil resistance.

35. **Jean-Jacques Rousseau (1712 – 78)** was a French philosopher and Enlightenment thinker, best known for his work on political philosophy, human nature, and education.

36. **Rudolph Rummel (1932 – 2014)** was a historian of violence, who specialized in genocides. He invented the term "democide" to talk about systematic murder by governmental forces.

37. **Todd K. Shackelford (b. 1971)** is an American evolutionary psychologist and professor at Oakland University.

38. **Peter Singer (b. 1946)** is an Australian-born philosopher and professor of bioethics at Princeton University. He specializes in moral philosophy and ethics and is best known for his work on animal rights.

39. **Nassim Nicholas Taleb (b. 1960)** is a Lebanese American statistician who specializes in studying randomness and probability. He is famous for his book *The Black Swan.*

40. **Bradley Alfred Thayer** is an associate professor of political science at the University of Minnesota Duluth. He wrote *Darwin and International Relations: On the Evolutionary Origins of War and Ethnic Conflict* (2004).

41. **John Tooby (b. 1952)** is an American anthropologist, best known for his work as an evolutionary psychologist, alongside his wife Leda Cosmides.

42. **Margo Wilson (1942 – 2009)** was a Canadian evolutionary psychologist, best known for her work on homicide and violence risk.

43. **Mark Zuckerberg (b. 1984)** is an American Internet entrepreneur, best known for being the founder of Facebook.

 WORKS CITED

1. Benjamin, Geoffrey, Robert K. Dentan, Charles MacDonald, Kirk M. Endicott, Otto Steinmayer, and Barbara S. Nowak. "Violence: Finding Peace." *Science* 338, no. 6105 (2012): 327.

2. Clark, Gregory. *A Farewell to Alms: A Brief Economic History of the World.* Princeton, NJ: Princeton University Press, 2008.

3. Cohen, Roger. "A Climate of Fear." *New York Times*, October 27, 2011. Accessed December 22, 2015. http://www.nytimes.com/2014/10/28/opinion/roger-cohen-a-climate-of-fear.html.

4. Daly, Martin, and Margo Wilson. *Homicide.* New Brunswick, NJ: Transaction Publishers, 1988.

5. Decety, Jean, and Jason M. Cowell. "The Complex Relation between Morality and Empathy." *Trends in Cognitive Sciences* 18, no. 7 (2014): 337–9.

6. Deutsch, David. *The Beginning of Infinity: Explanations That Transform the World.* London: Penguin, 2011.

7. Dugdale, John. "Richard Dawkins Named World's Top Thinker in Poll." *Guardian*, April 23, 2013. Accessed December 22, 2015. http://www.theguardian.com/books/booksblog/2013/apr/25/richard-dawkins-named-top-thinker.

8. Elias, Norbert. *The Civilizing Process.* Translated by Edmund Jephcott. New York: Pantheon Books, 1982.

9. Ellingson, Terry Jay. *The Myth of the Noble Savage.* Berkeley: University of California Press, 2001.

10. Gates, Bill. "The Better Angels of Our Nature: Why Violence Has Declined." *Gatesnotes*, June 12, 2012. Accessed December 22, 2015. http://www.gatesnotes.com/Books/The-Better-Angels-of-Our-Nature.

11. Gleditsch, Nils Petter, Steven Pinker, Bradley A. Thayer, Jack S. Levy, and William R. Thompson. "The Forum: The Decline of War." *International Studies Review* 15, no. 3 (2013): 396–419.

12. Goldstein, Joshua S. *Winning the War on War: The Decline of Armed Conflict Worldwide.* New York: Dutton/Plume (Penguin), 2011.

13. Gray, John. *Straw Dogs: Thoughts on Humans and Other Animals*. London: Granta, 2004.

14. ____. "Delusions of Peace." *Prospect* 21 (October 2011).

15. ____. "John Gray: Steven Pinker Is Wrong about Violence and War."

16. *Guardian*, March 15, 2015. Accessed December 22, 2015. http://www. theguardian.com/books/2015/mar/13/john-gray-steven-pinker-wrong-violence-war-declining.

17. Hobbes, Thomas. *Leviathan*. Oxford: Clarendon Press, 2012 (1651).

18. Jervis, Robert. "Pinker the Prophet." *National Interest*, Nov—Dec 2011. Accessed December 22, 2015. http://nationalinterest.org/bookreview/pinker-the-prophet-6072.

19. Nam C. Kim "Angels, Illusions, Hydras, and Chimeras: Violence and Humanity." *Reviews in Anthropology* 41, no. 4 (2012): 239–72.

20. Kohler, Timothy, Scott Ortman, Katie Grundtisch, Carly Fitzpatrick, and Sarah Cole. "The Better Angels of Their Nature: Declining Violence through Time among Prehispanic Farmers of the Pueblo Southwest." *American Antiquity* 79, no. 3 (July 1, 2014): 444–64. Accessed December 22, 2015. doi: 10.7183/0002-7316.79.3.444.

21. Kolbert, Elizabeth. "Peace in Our Time: Steven Pinker's History of Violence." *The New Yorker*, October 3, 2011. Accessed December 30, 2015. http://www. newyorker.com/magazine/2011/10/03/peace-in-our-time-elizabeth-kolbert.

22. Kosslyn, Stephen M., Steven Pinker, George E. Smith, and Steven P. Schwartz. "On the Demystification of Mental Imagery." *Behavioral and Brain Sciences* 2, no. 4 (1979): 535–81.

23. LaFree, Gary, Karise Curtis, and David McDowall. "How Effective Are Our 'The Better Angels'? Assessing Country-Level Declines in Homicide since 1950." *European Journal of Criminology* 12, no. 4 (2015): 482–504.

24. Muchembled, Robert. *A History of Violence: From the end of the Middle Ages to the Present*. Cambridge: Polity Press, 2012.

25. Mueller, John. "War Has Almost Ceased to Exist: An Assessment." *Political Science Quarterly* 124, no. 2 (2009): 297–321.

26. Paulson, Steve. "Proud Atheists." *Salon*, October 15, 2007. Accessed December 22, 2015. http://www.salon.com/2007/10/15/pinker_goldstein/.

27. Pinker, Steven. *How the Mind Works*. New York: Norton, 1997.

28. ____. "All About Evil." *New York Times*, October 29, 2000. Accessed December 22, 2015. http://www.nytimes.com/2000/10/29/books/all-about-evil.html.

29. ____. *The Blank Slate: The Modern Denial of Human Nature*. London: Penguin, 2003.

30. ____. *The Stuff of Thought: Language as a Window into Human Nature*. London: Penguin, 2007.

31. ____. "The Moral Instinct." *New York Times*, January 13, 2008. Accessed December 22, 2015. http://www.nytimes.com/2008/01/13/magazine/13Psychology-t.html?pagewanted=all&_r=0.

32. ____. *The Better Angels of Our Nature: The Decline of Violence in History and Its Causes*. London: Penguin, 2011.

33. ____. "Decline of Violence: Taming the Devil within Us." *Nature* 478, no. 7369 (2011): 309–11.

34. ____. *The Sense of Style: The Thinking Person's Guide to Writing in the 21st Century*. London: Penguin, 2014.

35. ____. "Steven Pinker: By the Book." *New York Times: The Sunday Book Review*, September 25, 2014. Accessed December 22, 2015. http://www.nytimes.com/2014/09/28/books/review/steven-pinker-by-the-book.html.

36. ____. "Graphic Evidence: Steven Pinker's Optimism on Trial." *Guardian*, September 11, 2015. Accessed December 22, 2015. http://www.theguardian.com/commentisfree/ng-interactive/2015/sep/11/graphic-evidence-steven-pinkers-optimism-on-trial.

37. ____. "Now for the Good News: Things Really Are Getting Better." *Guardian*,

September 11, 2015. Accessed December 29, 2015. http://www.theguardian. com/commentisfree/2015/sep/11/news-isis-syria-headlines-violence-steven- pinker

38. ____. "Frequently Asked Questions about *The Better Angels of Our Nature: Why Violence Has Declined*." Steven Pinker: Department of Psychology, Harvard University. Accessed December 22, 2015. http://stevenpinker.com/ pages/frequently-asked-questions-about-better-angels-our-nature-why-violence- has-declined.

39. ____. "Has the Decline of Violence Reversed Since *The Better Angels of Our Nature* Was Written?" Accessed December 22, 2015. http://stevenpinker.com/ files/pinker/files/has_the_decline_of_violence_reversed_since_the_better_ angels_of_our_nature_was_written.pdf.

40. ____. "Response to the Book Review Symposium: Steven Pinker, *The Better Angels of Our Nature*." *Sociology* 49, no.4 (2015): NP3–NP8.

41. ____. *Words and Rules: The Ingredients of Language*. New York: Basic Books, 2015.

42. Pinker, Steven, and Elizabeth Spelke. "The Science of Gender and Science. Pinker vs. Spelke." *Edge: The Third Culture*, May 16, 2005. Accessed December 22, 2015. http://edge.org/3rd_culture/debate05/debate05_index.html.

43. Ray, Larry, Lea John, Rose Hilary, and Bhatt Chetan. "Book Review Symposium: Steven Pinker, *The Better Angels of Our Nature: A History of Violence and Humanity*." *Sociology* 47, no. 6 (2013): 1224–32.

44. Richardson, Lewis Fry. *Statistics of Deadly Quarrels*. Edited by Quincy Wright and C. C. Lienau. Pittsburgh: Boxwood Press, 1960.

45. Roberts, Adam. "The Long Peace Getting Longer." *Survival* 54, no. 1 (2012): 175–84.

46. Rousseau, Jean-Jacques. *Discourse on the Origin of Inequality*. Translated by Franklin Philip. Oxford: Oxford's World Classics, 2009 (1755).

47. Rummel, Rudolph J. *Death by Government*. New Brunswick, NJ: Transaction Publishers, 1997.

48. Schmidt, Bettina, and Ingo Schröder. *Anthropology of Violence and Conflict.* New York: Routledge/Psychology Press, 2001.

49. Shackelford, Todd Kennedy, and Ranald D. Hansen. *The Evolution of Violence.* New York: Springer Verlag, 2014.

50. Singer, Peter. *The Expanding Circle.* Oxford: Clarendon Press, 1981.

51. ____. "Is Violence History?" *New York Times*, October 6, 2011. Accessed December 22, 2015. http://www.nytimes.com/2011/10/09/books/review/the-better-angels-of-our-nature-by-steven-pinker-book-review.html.

52. Taleb, Nassim Nicholas. Facebook entry, August 11, 2003. Accessed December 22, 2015. https: //www.facebook.com/permalink.php?story_fbid=101516419318 53375&id=13012333374

53. ____. "Fat Tails, Model Uncertainty and the Law of Very Large Numbers." Accessed December 22, 2015. http://exploredoc.com/doc/4907575/how-large-the-n%3F---nassim-nicholas-taleb.

54. ____. *The "Long Peace" Is a Statistical Illusion.* Accessed December 22, 2015. http://www.fooledbyrandomness.com/longpeace.pdf.

55. Tooby, John, and Leda Cosmides. "Groups in Mind: The Coalitional Roots of War and Morality." In *Human Morality and Sociality: Evolutionary and Comparative Perspectives*, edited by Henrik Hogh-Olesen, 91–234. New York: Palgrave Macmillan, 2010.

56. Viskontas, Indre, and Chris Mooney. "Steven Pinker on Violence." *Skeptical Inquirer* 37, no. 4 (August 2013). Accessed December 22, 2015. http://www.csicop.org/si/show/steven_pinker_on_violence/.

57. Zuckerberg, Mark. "A Year of Books." January 28, 2015, accessed December 30, 2015, https: //www.facebook.com/ayearofbooks/posts/831583243554273.

原书作者简介

斯蒂芬·平克十几岁时曾是一位无政府主义者。而今，他是世界知名的哈佛大学心理学教授、畅销书作者、认知科学的领军人物。平克于 1954 年生于加拿大，40 岁时出版了他的第一本畅销书——《语言本能》。该书探究了语言学家诺姆·乔姆斯基的观点，将其呈献给大众读者。平克的声誉随着其后续作品不断攀升，这些作品有《心智探奇》《白板》。但在 2011 年，随着《人性中的善良天使:暴力为什么会减少》问世，平克被誉为当今时代最重要的全球思想家之一。

本书作者简介

茱莉亚·斯莫尔奇科娃获巴黎让·尼科德研究所的社会心理学博士学位。该研究所是法国国家科学研究院（CNRS）位于巴黎的一家研究中心，由巴黎高等师范学院（ENS）、法国社会科学高等研究院（EHESS）共同主办。茱莉亚目前在德国波鸿鲁尔大学任博士后研究员。

世界名著中的批判性思维

《世界思想宝库钥匙丛书》致力于深入浅出地阐释全世界著名思想家的观点，不论是谁、在何处都能了解到，从而推进批判性思维发展。

《世界思想宝库钥匙丛书》与世界顶尖大学的一流学者合作，为一系列学科中最有影响的著作推出新的分析文本，介绍其观点和影响。在这一不断扩展的系列中，每种选入的著作都代表了历经时间考验的思想典范。通过为这些著作提供必要背景、揭示原作者的学术渊源以及说明这些著作所产生的影响，本系列图书希望让读者以新视角看待这些划时代的经典之作。读者应学会思考、运用并挑战这些著作中的观点，而不是简单接受它们。

ABOUT THE AUTHOR OF THE ORIGINAL WORK

Steven Pinker was a teenage anarchist. Today he is a world-renowned Harvard psychology professor, a best-selling author, and a leading cognitive scientist. Born in Canada in 1954, Pinker published his first best seller the year he turned 40. *The Language Instinct* explored the ideas of linguist Noam Chomsky and presented them to a popular audience. Pinker's reputation grew with his later books, including *HowThe MindWorks* and *The Blank Slate*. But it was in 2011, with the publication of *The Better Angels of Our Nature: WhyViolence Has Declined*, that he began to be heralded as one of the most important global thinkers of our time.

ABOUT THE AUTHOR OF THE ANALYSIS

Dr Joulia Smortchkova holds a PhD in social psychology from the Institut Jean Nicod (CNRS, ENS, EHESS), Paris. She is currently a Postdoctoral Fellow at the Ruhr-Universität Bochum.

ABOUT MACAT
GREAT WORKS FOR CRITICAL THINKING

Macat is focused on making the ideas of the world's great thinkers accessible and comprehensible to everybody, everywhere, in ways that promote the development of enhanced critical thinking skills.

It works with leading academics from the world's top universities to produce new analyses that focus on the ideas and the impact of the most influential works ever written across a wide variety of academic disciplines. Each of the works that sit at the heart of its growing library is an enduring example of great thinking. But by setting them in context — and looking at the influences that shaped their authors, as well as the responses they provoked — Macat encourages readers to look at these classics and game-changers with fresh eyes. Readers learn to think, engage and challenge their ideas, rather than simply accepting them.

批判性思维与《人性中的善良天使》

首要批判性思维技巧：理性化思维

次要批判性思维技巧：阐释

理性化思维是一种批判性思维技巧，它与论点的形成密切相关。理性化思维使得论点条理更加清晰、连贯、可靠，在必要情况下还能对相反论点作出回击。《人性中的善良天使》一步步详尽地展示了如何运用这些技巧。作者斯蒂芬·平克的核心论点十分直接：几个世纪以来，人类变得越来越不暴力，而且还将持续如此。然而，平克也意识到许多人会本能地反对这一观点。《人性中的善良天使》侧重以收集、整理数据的方式来支持、阐释其核心论点，以及一系列关于人类如何及因何变得不那么暴力的次要论点。随着平克着手应对那些错综复杂的数据，以及数据所呈现出的问题和人们作出的推断，他的阐释技巧——即参透历史所遗留下来的复杂证据——贯穿全书始终，发挥着重要的作用。

CRITICAL THINKING AND *THE BETTER ANGELS OF OUR NATURE*

• Primary critical thinking skill: REASONING

• Secondary critical thinking skill: INTERPRETATION

Reasoning is the critical thinking skill concerned with the production of arguments: making them coherent, consistent, and well-supported; and responding to opposing positions where necessary. *The Better Angels of Our Nature* offers a step-by-step class in precisely these skills. Author Steven Pinker's central thesis is simple: mankind has become increasingly less violent over the centuries, and will continue to do so. Pinker is aware, though, that many people instinctively believe the opposite, and *Better Angels* is devoted to marshalling data to support and illustrate this central argument, as well as a series of secondary arguments about how and why humanity has become less violent. Pinker's interpretative skills — understanding the meaning of the complex evidence from history — are also on display throughout, as he tackles the ambiguities of his data, the problems it presents, and the viable inferences one can draw from it.

《世界思想宝库钥匙丛书》简介

《世界思想宝库钥匙丛书》致力于为一系列在各领域产生重大影响的人文社科类经典著作提供独特的学术探讨。每一本读物都不仅仅是原经典著作的内容摘要，而是介绍并深入研究原经典著作的学术渊源、主要观点和历史影响。这一丛书的目的是提供一套学习资料，以促进读者掌握批判性思维，从而更全面、深刻地去理解重要思想。

每一本读物分为 3 个部分：学术渊源、学术思想和学术影响，每个部分下有 4 个小节。这些章节旨在从各个方面研究原经典著作及其反响。

由于独特的体例，每一本读物不但易于阅读，而且另有一项优点：所有读物的编排体例相同，读者在进行某个知识层面的调查或研究时可交叉参阅多本该丛书中的相关读物，从而开启跨领域研究的路径。

为了方便阅读，每本读物最后还列出了术语表和人名表（在书中则以星号 * 标记），此外还有参考文献。

《世界思想宝库钥匙丛书》与剑桥大学合作，理清了批判性思维的要点，即如何通过 6 种技能来进行有效思考。其中 3 种技能让我们能够理解问题，另 3 种技能让我们有能力解决问题。这 6 种技能合称为"批判性思维 PACIER 模式"，它们是：

分析：了解如何建立一个观点；

评估：研究一个观点的优点和缺点；

阐释：对意义所产生的问题加以理解；

创造性思维：提出新的见解，发现新的联系；

解决问题：提出切实有效的解决办法；

理性化思维：创建有说服力的观点。

THE MACAT LIBRARY

The Macat Library is a series of unique academic explorations of seminal works in the humanities and social sciences — books and papers that have had a significant and widely recognised impact on their disciplines. It has been created to serve as much more than just a summary of what lies between the covers of a great book. It illuminates and explores the influences on, ideas of, and impact of that book. Our goal is to offer a learning resource that encourages critical thinking and fosters a better, deeper understanding of important ideas.

Each publication is divided into three Sections: Influences, Ideas, and Impact. Each Section has four Modules. These explore every important facet of the work, and the responses to it.

This Section-Module structure makes a Macat Library book easy to use, but it has another important feature. Because each Macat book is written to the same format, it is possible (and encouraged!) to cross-reference multiple Macat books along the same lines of inquiry or research. This allows the reader to open up interesting interdisciplinary pathways.

To further aid your reading, lists of glossary terms and people mentioned are included at the end of this book (these are indicated by an asterisk [*] throughout) — as well as a list of works cited.

Macat has worked with the University of Cambridge to identify the elements of critical thinking and understand the ways in which six different skills combine to enable effective thinking.

Three allow us to fully understand a problem; three more give us the tools to solve it. Together, these six skills make up the PACIER model of critical thinking. They are:

ANALYSIS — understanding how an argument is built
EVALUATION — exploring the strengths and weaknesses of an argument
INTERPRETATION — understanding issues of meaning
CREATIVE THINKING — coming up with new ideas and fresh connections
PROBLEM-SOLVING — producing strong solutions
REASONING — creating strong arguments

"《世界思想宝库钥匙丛书》提供了独一无二的跨学科学习和研究工具。它介绍那些革新了各自学科研究的经典著作，还邀请全世界一流专家和教育机构进行严谨的分析，为每位读者打开世界顶级教育的大门。"

—— 安德烈亚斯·施莱歇尔，
经济合作与发展组织教育与技能司司长

"《世界思想宝库钥匙丛书》直面大学教育的巨大挑战……他们组建了一支精干而活跃的学者队伍，来推出在研究广度上颇具新意的教学材料。"

—— 布罗尔斯教授、勋爵，剑桥大学前校长

"《世界思想宝库钥匙丛书》的愿景令人赞叹。它通过分析和阐释那些曾深刻影响人类思想以及社会、经济发展的经典文本，提供了新的学习方法。它推动批判性思维，这对于任何社会和经济体来说都是至关重要的。这就是未来的学习方法。"

—— 查尔斯·克拉克阁下，英国前教育大臣

"对于那些影响了各自领域的著作，《世界思想宝库钥匙丛书》能让人们立即了解到围绕那些著作展开的评论性言论，这让该系列图书成为在这些领域从事研究的师生们不可或缺的资源。"

—— 威廉·特朗佐教授，加利福尼亚大学圣地亚哥分校

"Macat offers an amazing first-of-its-kind tool for interdisciplinary learning and research. Its focus on works that transformed their disciplines and its rigorous approach, drawing on the world's leading experts and educational institutions, opens up a world-class education to anyone."

—— Andreas Schleicher, Director for Education and Skills, Organisation for Economic Co-operation and Development

"Macat is taking on some of the major challenges in university education... They have drawn together a strong team of active academics who are producing teaching materials that are novel in the breadth of their approach."

—— Prof Lord Broers, former Vice-Chancellor of the University of Cambridge

"The Macat vision is exceptionally exciting. It focuses upon new modes of learning which analyse and explain seminal texts which have profoundly influenced world thinking and so social and economic development. It promotes the kind of critical thinking which is essential for any society and economy. This is the learning of the future."

—— Rt Hon Charles Clarke, former UK Secretary of State for Education

"The Macat analyses provide immediate access to the critical conversation surrounding the books that have shaped their respective discipline, which will make them an invaluable resource to all of those, students and teachers, working in the field."

—— Prof William Tronzo, University of California at San Diego

♀ The Macat Library
世界思想宝库钥匙丛书

TITLE	中文书名	类别
An Analysis of Arjun Appadurai's *Modernity at Large: Cultural Dimensions of Globalization*	解析阿尔君·阿帕杜莱《消失的现代性：全球化的文化维度》	人类学
An Analysis of Claude Lévi-Strauss's *Structural Anthropology*	解析克劳德·列维-斯特劳斯《结构人类学》	人类学
An Analysis of Marcel Mauss's *The Gift*	解析马塞尔·莫斯《礼物》	人类学
An Analysis of Jared M. Diamond's *Guns, Germs, and Steel: The Fate of Human Societies*	解析贾雷德·M.戴蒙德《枪炮、病菌与钢铁：人类社会的命运》	人类学
An Analysis of Clifford Geertz's *The Interpretation of Cultures*	解析克利福德·格尔茨《文化的解释》	人类学
An Analysis of Philippe Ariès's *Centuries of Childhood: A Social History of Family Life*	解析菲力浦·阿利埃斯《儿童的世纪：旧制度下的儿童和家庭生活》	人类学
An Analysis of W. Chan Kim & Renée Mauborgne's *Blue Ocean Strategy*	解析金伟灿/勒妮·莫博涅《蓝海战略》	商业
An Analysis of John P. Kotter's *Leading Change*	解析约翰·P.科特《领导变革》	商业
An Analysis of Michael E. Porter's *Competitive Strategy: Techniques for Analyzing Industries and Competitors*	解析迈克尔·E.波特《竞争战略：分析产业和竞争对手的技术》	商业
An Analysis of Jean Lave & Etienne Wenger's *Situated Learning: Legitimate Peripheral Participation*	解析琼·莱夫/艾蒂纳·温格《情境学习：合法的边缘性参与》	商业
An Analysis of Douglas McGregor's *The Human Side of Enterprise*	解析道格拉斯·麦格雷戈《企业的人性面》	商业
An Analysis of Milton Friedman's *Capitalism and Freedom*	解析米尔顿·弗里德曼《资本主义与自由》	商业
An Analysis of Ludwig von Mises's *The Theory of Money and Credit*	解析路德维希·冯·米塞斯《货币和信用理论》	经济学
An Analysis of Adam Smith's *The Wealth of Nations*	解析亚当·斯密《国富论》	经济学
An Analysis of Thomas Piketty's *Capital in the Twenty-First Century*	解析托马斯·皮凯蒂《21世纪资本论》	经济学
An Analysis of Nassim Nicholas Taleb's *The Black Swan: The Impact of the Highly Improbable*	解析纳西姆·尼古拉斯·塔勒布《黑天鹅：如何应对不可预知的未来》	经济学
An Analysis of Ha-Joon Chang's *Kicking Away the Ladder*	解析张夏准《富国陷阱：发达国家为何踢开梯子》	经济学
An Analysis of Thomas Robert Malthus's *An Essay on the Principle of Population*	解析托马斯·罗伯特·马尔萨斯《人口论》	经济学

An Analysis of John Maynard Keynes's *The General Theory of Employment, Interest and Money*	解析约翰·梅纳德·凯恩斯《就业、利息和货币通论》	经济学
An Analysis of Milton Friedman's *The Role of Monetary Policy*	解析米尔顿·弗里德曼《货币政策的作用》	经济学
An Analysis of Burton G. Malkiel's *A Random Walk Down Wall Street*	解析伯顿·G.马尔基尔《漫步华尔街》	经济学
An Analysis of Friedrich A. Hayek's *The Road to Serfdom*	解析弗里德里希·A.哈耶克《通往奴役之路》	经济学
An Analysis of Charles P. Kindleberger's *Manias, Panics, and Crashes: A History of Financial Crises*	解析查尔斯·P.金德尔伯格《疯狂、惊恐和崩溃：金融危机史》	经济学
An Analysis of Amartya Sen's *Development as Freedom*	解析阿马蒂亚·森《以自由看待发展》	经济学
An Analysis of Rachel Carson's *Silent Spring*	解析蕾切尔·卡森《寂静的春天》	地理学
An Analysis of Charles Darwin's *On the Origin of Species: by Means of Natural Selection, or The Preservation of Favoured Races in the Struggle for Life*	解析查尔斯·达尔文《物种起源》	地理学
An Analysis of World Commission on Environment and Development's *The Brundtland Report: Our Common Future*	解析世界环境与发展委员会《布伦特兰报告：我们共同的未来》	地理学
An Analysis of James E. Lovelock's *Gaia: A New Look at Life on Earth*	解析詹姆斯·E.拉伍洛克《盖娅：地球生命的新视野》	地理学
An Analysis of Paul Kennedy's *The Rise and Fall of the Great Powers: Economic Change and Military Conflict from 1500–2000*	解析保罗·肯尼迪《大国的兴衰：1500—2000年的经济变革与军事冲突》	历史
An Analysis of Janet L. Abu-Lughod's *Before European Hegemony: The World System A. D. 1250–1350*	解析珍妮特·L.阿布-卢格霍德《欧洲霸权之前：1250—1350年的世界体系》	历史
An Analysis of Alfred W. Crosby's *The Columbian Exchange: Biological and Cultural Consequences of 1492*	解析艾尔弗雷德·W.克罗斯比《哥伦布大交换：1492年以后的生物影响和文化冲击》	历史
An Analysis of Tony Judt's *Postwar: A History of Europe since 1945*	解析托尼·朱特《战后欧洲史》	历史
An Analysis of Richard J. Evans's *In Defence of History*	解析理查德·J.艾文斯《捍卫历史》	历史
An Analysis of Eric Hobsbawm's *The Age of Revolution: Europe 1789–1848*	解析艾瑞克·霍布斯鲍姆《革命的年代：欧洲1789—1848年》	历史

An Analysis of Roland Barthes's *Mythologies*	解析罗兰·巴特《神话学》	文学与批判理论
An Analysis of Simone de Beauvoir's *The Second Sex*	解析西蒙娜·德·波伏娃《第二性》	文学与批判理论
An Analysis of Edward W. Said's *Orientalism*	解析爱德华·W.萨义德《东方主义》	文学与批判理论
An Analysis of Virginia Woolf's *A Room of One's Own*	解析弗吉尼亚·伍尔芙《一间自己的房间》	文学与批判理论
An Analysis of Judith Butler's *Gender Trouble*	解析朱迪斯·巴特勒《性别麻烦》	文学与批判理论
An Analysis of Ferdinand de Saussure's *Course in General Linguistics*	解析费尔迪南·德·索绪尔《普通语言学教程》	文学与批判理论
An Analysis of Susan Sontag's *On Photography*	解析苏珊·桑塔格《论摄影》	文学与批判理论
An Analysis of Walter Benjamin's *The Work of Art in the Age of Mechanical Reproduction*	解析瓦尔特·本雅明《机械复制时代的艺术作品》	文学与批判理论
An Analysis of W. E. B. Du Bois's *The Souls of Black Folk*	解析W.E.B.杜波依斯《黑人的灵魂》	文学与批判理论
An Analysis of Plato's *The Republic*	解析柏拉图《理想国》	哲学
An Analysis of Plato's *Symposium*	解析柏拉图《会饮篇》	哲学
An Analysis of Aristotle's *Metaphysics*	解析亚里士多德《形而上学》	哲学
An Analysis of Aristotle's *Nicomachean Ethics*	解析亚里士多德《尼各马可伦理学》	哲学
An Analysis of Immanuel Kant's *Critique of Pure Reason*	解析伊曼努尔·康德《纯粹理性批判》	哲学
An Analysis of Ludwig Wittgenstein's *Philosophical Investigations*	解析路德维希·维特根斯坦《哲学研究》	哲学
An Analysis of G. W. F. Hegel's *Phenomenology of Spirit*	解析G.W.F.黑格尔《精神现象学》	哲学
An Analysis of Baruch Spinoza's *Ethics*	解析巴鲁赫·斯宾诺莎《伦理学》	哲学
An Analysis of Hannah Arendt's *The Human Condition*	解析汉娜·阿伦特《人的境况》	哲学
An Analysis of G. E. M. Anscombe's *Modern Moral Philosophy*	解析G.E.M.安斯康姆《现代道德哲学》	哲学
An Analysis of David Hume's *An Enquiry Concerning Human Understanding*	解析大卫·休谟《人类理解研究》	哲学

An Analysis of Søren Kierkegaard's *Fear and Trembling*	解析索伦·克尔凯郭尔《恐惧与战栗》	哲学
An Analysis of René Descartes's *Meditations on First Philosophy*	解析勒内·笛卡尔《第一哲学沉思录》	哲学
An Analysis of Friedrich Nietzsche's *On the Genealogy of Morality*	解析弗里德里希·尼采《论道德的谱系》	哲学
An Analysis of Gilbert Ryle's *The Concept of Mind*	解析吉尔伯特·赖尔《心的概念》	哲学
An Analysis of Thomas Kuhn's *The Structure of Scientific Revolutions*	解析托马斯·库恩《科学革命的结构》	哲学
An Analysis of John Stuart Mill's *Utilitarianism*	解析约翰·斯图亚特·穆勒《功利主义》	哲学
An Analysis of Aristotle's *Politics*	解析亚里士多德《政治学》	政治学
An Analysis of Niccolò Machiavelli's *The Prince*	解析尼科洛·马基雅维利《君主论》	政治学
An Analysis of Karl Marx's *Capital*	解析卡尔·马克思《资本论》	政治学
An Analysis of Benedict Anderson's *Imagined Communities*	解析本尼迪克特·安德森《想象的共同体》	政治学
An Analysis of Samuel P. Huntington's *The Clash of Civilizations and the Remaking of World Order*	解析塞缪尔·P.亨廷顿《文明的冲突与世界秩序的重建》	政治学
An Analysis of Alexis de Tocqueville's *Democracy in America*	解析阿列克西·德·托克维尔《论美国的民主》	政治学
An Analysis of John A. Hobson's *Imperialism: A Study*	解析约翰·A.霍布森《帝国主义》	政治学
An Analysis of Thomas Paine's *Common Sense*	解析托马斯·潘恩《常识》	政治学
An Analysis of John Rawls's *A Theory of Justice*	解析约翰·罗尔斯《正义论》	政治学
An Analysis of Francis Fukuyama's *The End of History and the Last Man*	解析弗朗西斯·福山《历史的终结与最后的人》	政治学
An Analysis of John Locke's *Two Treatises of Government*	解析约翰·洛克《政府论》	政治学
An Analysis of Sun Tzu's *The Art of War*	解析孙武《孙子兵法》	政治学
An Analysis of Henry Kissinger's *World Order: Reflections on the Character of Nations and the Course of History*	解析亨利·基辛格《世界秩序》	政治学
An Analysis of Jean-Jacques Rousseau's *The Social Contract*	解析让-雅克·卢梭《社会契约论》	政治学

An Analysis of Odd Arne Westad's *The Global Cold War: Third World Interventions and the Making of Our Times*	解析文安立《全球冷战：美苏对第三世界的干涉与当代世界的形成》	政治学
An Analysis of Sigmund Freud's *The Interpretation of Dreams*	解析西格蒙德·弗洛伊德《梦的解析》	心理学
An Analysis of William James' *The Principles of Psychology*	解析威廉·詹姆斯《心理学原理》	心理学
An Analysis of Philip Zimbardo's *The Lucifer Effect*	解析菲利普·津巴多《路西法效应》	心理学
An Analysis of Leon Festinger's *A Theory of Cognitive Dissonance*	解析利昂·费斯汀格《认知失调论》	心理学
An Analysis of Richard H. Thaler & Cass R. Sunstein's *Nudge: Improving Decisions about Health, Wealth, and Happiness*	解析理查德·H. 泰勒／卡斯·R. 桑斯坦《助推：如何做出有关健康、财富和幸福的更优决策》	心理学
An Analysis of Gordon Allport's *The Nature of Prejudice*	解析高尔登·奥尔波特《偏见的本质》	心理学
An Analysis of Steven Pinker's *The Better Angels of Our Nature: Why Violence Has Declined*	解析斯蒂芬·平克《人性中的善良天使：暴力为什么会减少》	心理学
An Analysis of Stanley Milgram's *Obedience to Authority*	解析斯坦利·米尔格拉姆《对权威的服从》	心理学
An Analysis of Betty Friedan's *The Feminine Mystique*	解析贝蒂·弗里丹《女性的奥秘》	心理学
An Analysis of David Riesman's *The Lonely Crowd: A Study of the Changing American Character*	解析大卫·理斯曼《孤独的人群：美国人社会性格演变之研究》	社会学
An Analysis of Franz Boas's *Race, Language and Culture*	解析弗朗兹·博厄斯《种族、语言与文化》	社会学
An Analysis of Pierre Bourdieu's *Outline of a Theory of Practice*	解析皮埃尔·布尔迪厄《实践理论大纲》	社会学
An Analysis of Max Weber's *The Protestant Ethic and the Spirit of Capitalism*	解析马克斯·韦伯《新教伦理与资本主义精神》	社会学
An Analysis of Jane Jacobs's *The Death and Life of Great American Cities*	解析简·雅各布斯《美国大城市的死与生》	社会学
An Analysis of C. Wright Mills's *The Sociological Imagination*	解析 C. 赖特·米尔斯《社会学的想象力》	社会学
An Analysis of Robert E. Lucas Jr.'s *Why Doesn't Capital Flow from Rich to Poor Countries?*	解析小罗伯特·E. 卢卡斯《为何资本不从富国流向穷国？》	社会学

An Analysis of Émile Durkheim's *On Suicide*	解析埃米尔·迪尔凯姆《自杀论》	社会学
An Analysis of Eric Hoffer's *The True Believer: Thoughts on the Nature of Mass Movements*	解析埃里克·霍弗《狂热分子：群众运动圣经》	社会学
An Analysis of Jared M. Diamond's *Collapse: How Societies Choose to Fail or Survive*	解析贾雷德·M.戴蒙德《大崩溃：社会如何选择兴亡》	社会学
An Analysis of Michel Foucault's *The History of Sexuality Vol. 1: The Will to Knowledge*	解析米歇尔·福柯《性史（第一卷）：求知意志》	社会学
An Analysis of Michel Foucault's *Discipline and Punish*	解析米歇尔·福柯《规训与惩罚》	社会学
An Analysis of Richard Dawkins's *The Selfish Gene*	解析理查德·道金斯《自私的基因》	社会学
An Analysis of Antonio Gramsci's *Prison Notebooks*	解析安东尼奥·葛兰西《狱中札记》	社会学
An Analysis of Augustine's *Confessions*	解析奥古斯丁《忏悔录》	神学
An Analysis of C. S. Lewis's *The Abolition of Man*	解析 C. S. 路易斯《人之废》	神学

图书在版编目（CIP）数据

解析斯蒂芬·平克《人性中的善良天使》/ 茱莉亚·斯莫尔奇科娃
（Joulia Smortchkova）著；乔洁译 . —上海：上海外语教育出版社，
2021
（世界思想宝库钥匙丛书）
ISBN 978-7-5446-6756-2

Ⅰ.①解… Ⅱ.①茱… ②乔… Ⅲ.①世界史－文化史－研究 Ⅳ.
①K103

中国版本图书馆CIP数据核字（2021）第042961号

This Chinese-English bilingual edition of *An Analysis of Steven Pinker's* The Better Angels of Our Nature is published by arrangement with Macat International Limited.
Licensed for sale throughout the world.

本书汉英双语版由Macat国际有限公司授权上海外语教育出版社有限公司出版。
供在全世界范围内发行、销售。

图字：09 – 2018 – 549

出版发行：上海外语教育出版社
（上海外国语大学内） 邮编：200083
电　　话：021-65425300（总机）
电子邮箱：bookinfo@sflep.com.cn
网　　址：http://www.sflep.com
责任编辑：李振荣

印　　刷：上海叶大印务发展有限公司
开　　本：890×1240 1/32 印张 5.875 字数 121千字
版　　次：2021 年 8月第 1版 2021 年 8月第 1次印刷

书　　号：ISBN 978-7-5446-6756-2
定　　价：30.00 元

本版图书如有印装质量问题，可向本社调换
质量服务热线：4008-213-263 电子邮箱：editorial@sflep.com